Sequoia and Kings Canyon

A Guide to Sequoia and Kings Canyon
National Parks
California

Produced by the
Division of Publications
National Park Service

U.S. Department of the Interior
Washington, D.C.

Using This Handbook
Sequoia and Kings Canyon National Parks protect
giant sequoia trees and peaks and valleys of the
southern Sierra Nevada. Part 1 of this handbook
introduces the parks and their natural and cultural
values. Part 2 explores the rivers and canyons, the big
trees, and the mountain backcountry in both narrative text and graphic displays. Part 3 presents concise
travel guide and reference materials for touring the
parks, taking advantage of their programs and facilities, and camping.

National Park Handbooks are published to support
the National Park Service's management programs
and to promote understanding and enjoyment of the
more than 350 National Park System sites, which
represent important examples of our country's natural and cultural inheritance. Each handbook is intended to be informative reading before, during, and
after a park visit. More than 100 titles are in print.
They are sold at parks and can be purchased by mail
from the Superintendent of Documents, U.S. Government Printing Office, Washington, DC 20402. This
is handbook number 145.

Part 1 **Welcome to Sequoia and Kings Canyon 8**
Wild Nature Preserved for Its Own Sake 11

Part 2 **Landscapes of Superlatives 30**
Rivers and Canyons: Wilderness Before Its Time 33
The Big Trees: What Is Natural? 61
The High Mountains: Backcountry Choices 85

Part 3 **Guide and Adviser 104**
Approaching Sequoia and Kings Canyon 106
Map of the Parks 108
General Information 110
Visitor Centers, Exhibits, Interpretive Activities 111
Lodgings, Food Services, Campgrounds 114
Walking, Hiking, Backpacking, Wilderness Basics 116
Winter Activities 120
Fishing 122
Management Concerns, Safety Tips 123
Other Sierran National Park Areas 124
Armchair Explorations 125

Index 126

Part.1

Welcome to Sequoia
And Kings Canyon

Wild Nature Preserved
For Its Own Sake

Moro Rock juts from the edge of the Giant Forest, affording views of the Kaweah River canyon and Great Western Divide. Steps and railings enable visitors to avail themselves of stunning Sierran scenery from atop this granite dome. **Front cover and pages 8-9:** *As though on the toe of a Titan, children take true measure of one of the world's largest living things. The parks protect the giant sequoias — and project the possibility of such awe to future generations of children.* **Pages 2-3:** *High peaks catch and hold low-angled light rays in eastern Kings Canyon National Park.* **Pages 4-5:** *A giant sequoia dwarfs the Generals Highway.* **Pages 6-7:** *a small lake reflects Center Peak and Mount Stanford in Kings Canyon National Park.*

John Muir had inadvertently worked himself out onto smooth rock by an avalanche channel. He could go neither right nor left. He must go back or keep climbing. Going back looked more surely fatal. Muir pressed on: "After gaining a point about halfway to the top, I was suddenly brought to a dead stop, with arms outspread, clinging close to the face of the rock, unable to move hand or foot either up or down. My doom appeared fixed. I *must* fall. There would be a moment of bewilderment, and then a lifeless rumble down the one general precipice to the glacier below. . . .

"When this final danger flashed upon me," Muir later wrote, "I became nerve-shaken for the first time since setting foot on the mountain, and my mind seemed to fill with a stifling smoke. But this terrible eclipse lasted only a moment, when life blazed forth again with preternatural clearness. I seemed suddenly to become possessed of a new sense."

Muir instantly appreciated the import of this new sense — it would save his life. Moreover, at least two of Muir's literary biographers, Michael Cohen and Thomas J. Lyon, pinpoint this new sense as an awakened consciousness in Muir. Muir had entered, in Cohen's phrase, the primal consciousness of knowing by participation. It was a potent way of knowledge, pregnant with respect for the natural world, and very much at odds with our then young Nation's passion for rapid industrialization.

"Then my trembling muscles became firm again, every rift and flaw in the rock was seen as through a microscope, and my limbs moved with a positiveness and precision with which I seemed to have nothing at all to do."

The dividing line between Muir's self and outer nature had been, if not erased, greatly diminished. "Had I been borne aloft upon wings," he reflected, "my deliverance could not have been more complete." He also noted a strange influx of strength that

11

Preceding pages: *Blossoms*
of the shooting star provide
an ephemeral counterpoint
to a rugged backdrop of time-
worn rock.

"seemed inexhaustible. I found a way without effort, and soon stood upon the topmost crag in the blessed light." The year was 1872 and Muir's sensibilities had been incubating in the Sierran wilds of Yosemite since 1869.

The next year, 1873, John Muir left Yosemite and headed south along the Sierra. There he encountered the ultimate realm of the giant sequoias and marveled at the stupendous, human-dwarfing depths of Kings Canyon. Ultimately these wonders led Muir to envision a great southern Sierra national park encompassing the Big Trees, Kings Canyon, and Mt. Whitney.

All who love wild nature are still trying, in many respects, to catch-up with this 19th-century parkland and wilderness prophet. Not until 106 years after his curious identification with Sierran bedrock would we manage to approach—in 1978—Muir's envisioned park boundaries.

Today's phrase, "Welcome to Sequoia and Kings Canyon National Parks," encompasses more than 100 years of effort. Dates and bare facts alone obscure the years and sometimes decades of plot, counterplot, controversy, and compromise in the intensely human drama that established today's great southern Sierra national parks. The passage of time also obscures the fact that no national park tradition existed to guide and nurture these early, bold moves to protect wild nature with its deep canyons, big trees, and high peaks.

Fully told, the story of Sequoia and Kings Canyon National Parks includes much of the earliest history of national parks. At these parklands' birth, as General Grant and Sequoia national parks in 1890, creation of the National Park Service itself still stood a quarter-century in the future. Moreover, despite the fact that both parks have been in existence now for 100 years, we still may not claim rightly that they are preserved in perpetuity as Congress so clearly intended. It turns out that these parks are not island-like in enjoying a carefree isolation from the problems and pressures of our modern, technological lifeways. They are but parts of a larger ecosystem that includes San Joaquin Valley air pollution as well as the world's largest living things, the highest mountain in the contiguous states, and one of North

America's deepest canyons. As such, these parks can only be said to be preserved *for now* — so far, so good. Their preservation is a mandate without end. This realization — which is a new corrective to traditional thinking about our national parks — also makes each of us today just as important as were those who figured in the parks' first century.

Sensitivity to the special character of the Big Trees led in 1880 to the withdrawal from sale by the General Land Office of four sections (four square miles) of land around the General Grant Tree. In 1883 the Mt. Whitney Military Reservation was created, protecting the highest point in the contiguous United States — 14,494 feet above sea level — largely for scientific purposes. On September 25, 1890, a relatively small park was created to protect the forest watershed for San Joaquin Valley agriculture and to conserve the area's scenic and recreational values. One week later the park was expanded to about one-third its present size and named Sequoia National Park. The same legislation created General Grant (now part of Kings Canyon National Park) and Yosemite national parks. In 1926 Sequoia National Park was again expanded east to the Sierra crest including Mt. Whitney and the glacially carved Kern Canyon. In 1940 Kings Canyon National Park was created, but it protected only the spectacular mountain backcountry. Twenty five years later Kings Canyon National Park finally was expanded to include the awesome Kings Canyon and Tehipite Valley. The most recent major addition came in 1978 with Mineral King's inclusion in Sequoia National Park. And so we have arrived, as in assembling a puzzle, at the parklands approaching what John Muir envisioned and to which, in one breath, you may be welcomed today.

"Values," says Wallace Stegner, "both those that we approve and those that we don't, have roots as deep as creosote rings, and live as long, and grow as slowly." The players in this episodic, 100-year drama of creating Sequoia and Kings Canyon National Parks collectively tracked our Nation's evolving thinking about wild nature and its values.

With the 1880 withdrawal of land around the General Grant Tree, 19th-century America's fetish for natural oddities — preferably *big* ones — found a manifestation. This so-called esthetic of monumen-

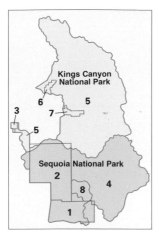

This map shows the evolution of the two parks: **1.** *A park to protect giant sequoias and Sierran watersheds was established in 1890.* **2.** *One week later it was trebled in size;* **3.** *General Grant National Park was established simultaneously.* **4.** *In 1926 Sequoia National Park more than doubled in size.* **5.** *In 1940 Kings Canyon National Park was established, incorporating General Grant National Park. It was expanded in 1965 to include* **6.** *parts of Tehipite Valley and* **7.** *Kings Canyon.* **8.** *In 1978, Congress added Mineral King to Sequoia National Park.*

talism arose from our emerging Nation's cultural insecurity. Feeling a lack of distinctive literature, arts, or other cultural accomplishments, we sought instead impressive natural monuments. Perhaps these could compete with Europe's imposing antiquities to win us coveted European respect. Giant sequoias, the world's largest living things—"vegetable Titans" they were called—were naturals for monumentalism. So too was Mt. Whitney.

By 1890, with creation of Sequoia National Park, this monumentalism had already mixed with a new and growing gospel of wise use: utilitarian conservation. In Part 2 of this handbook we witness Visalia newspaperman Col. George Stewart—himself loving nature in all its sizes—forming a coalition of park advocates among big tree lovers (monumentalists) and tourism boosters and agriculturalists (utilitarian conservationists). Park protection for giant sequoias resulted in part from a locally motivated campaign to protect the watersheds of San Joaquin Valley agriculture. Colonel Stewart loved the giant sequoias; he also understood politics.

But with the 1926 expansion of Sequoia National Park eastward to Mt. Whitney, preservation of nature became the driving motive. The creation of Kings Canyon National Park in 1940 marked a major commitment to preserving wilderness a quarter-century before passage of the 1964 Wilderness Act. And then in 1965, utilitarian conservation's pragmatic philosophy was soundly rejected—for these parks' purposes—as the entire Kings Canyon and Tehipite Valley finally were included in the park already named Kings Canyon. They had been excluded in 1940 because of their hydroelectric potential.

The dramatic shift in motive for preserving natural landscapes came in 1978 with the addition of Mineral King to Sequoia National Park. This addition followed a protracted legal battle over whether a major ski resort proposed by the Disney Corporation should be built on Sequoia Game Refuge lands then managed by the Forest Service of the U.S. Department of Agriculture. In an astonishing dissent to the U.S. Supreme Court's ruling that environmental groups lacked legal standing to pursue their case, Associate Justice William O. Douglas argued, with judicial precedents, that the trees themselves should have the right to sue for their protection.

That the law should recognize rights for natural objects was indeed a new notion. Pursuit of that concept has led us now to public discussion of bio-ethics: can we not base our moral judgments, particularly about complex environmental questions, on rights of nature and not on exclusively human-centered values?

As a land-use concept, national parks continue to evolve even as we approach the 21st century. Despite our earlier notions, we can no longer consider them island-like samples of wild nature protected from our urban industrial way of life. Parks are parts of larger wholes. The fates of Sequoia and Kings Canyon National Parks, for example, are inextricably linked with those of California and its San Joaquin Valley.

In 1984 Congress designated 85 percent of Sequoia and Kings Canyon National Parks as wilderness. The parks were named a Biosphere Reserve in 1976. **Pages 22-23:** *Clouds filter through Arc Pass on the eastern boundary of Sequoia National Park but leave Mt. Whitney unobscured on the near left skyline.* **Pages 24-25:** *Palisades Creek gathers in the Palisades, a group of peaks on the Sierra Crest along the eastern boundary of Kings Canyon National Park.*

In John Muir's early Sierran days the scientific view of nature was just beginning its rapid rise toward the space explorations and biogenetics of our own day. Interpretations of Charles Darwin's theory that an evolutionary mechanism explained the origin of species were challenging widely accepted creationist interpretations of nature. Together, the world view of science and social interpretations of Darwin's thought were feeding the political influence of utilitarian conservation as the 19th century drew to a close. The phrase "the greatest good for the greatest number" encapsulated its goals: we should manage natural resources for the best economic use to benefit the most people. This was the mindset of natural resources disposition, use, and management in the late-1800s.

This developing mindset had been surprised by creation of Yellowstone National Park in 1872 as a pleasuring ground. This was also the mindset that John Muir fought against so earnestly late in his life. Scientific though utilitarian conservation might be, it nevertheless contained the residue of the Christian religious assumption that Muir found himself increasingly unwilling to accept:

"The world, we are told, was made especially for man—a presumption not supported by all the facts," Muir had written in an early journal. "A numerous class of men are painfully astonished whenever they find anything, living or dead, in all God's universe, which they cannot eat or render in some way what they call useful to themselves." He later elaborated:

21

"No dogma taught by the present civilization seems to form so insuperable an obstacle in the way of a right understanding of the relations which culture sustains to wildness as that which regards the world as made especially for the uses of man."

John of the Mountains opted rather for acknowledging that "we all travel the milky way together, trees and men. . . ." Wild nature should be preserved for its own sake. It was a view that only time—our time—would bring any measure of popularity.

Writing about "the long road the nation traveled to get to Earth Day 1970," Wallace Stegner said that "Those who led us down it, the countless individuals and scores of organizations who resisted the lunchbucket and 'American initiative' arguments of resource exploiters, did not leave us a bad legacy." Nor did those who saw us through the first century of these two great parklands. Now it is up to us to be equally resolute about whatever problems may confront the big trees, wildlife, deep canyons, and high peaks of Sequoia and Kings Canyon National Parks. Such is our task implicit in Stegner's reflection that "Environmentalism or conservation or preservation, or whatever it should be called, is not a fact, and never has been. It is a job."

Part 2

Landscapes of Superlatives

Rivers and Canyons: Wilderness Before Its Time

Just outside Kings Canyon National Park, the South Fork of the Kings River cuts one of North America's deepest canyons. **Preceding pages:** *Evening sunlight bathes Mount Huxley in Kings Canyon National Park.*

John Muir found his ultimate canyon in Kings Canyon in 1873: "It is about ten miles long, half a mile wide, and the stupendous rocks of purplish gray granite that form the walls are from 2500 to 5000 feet in height, while the depth of the valley below the general surface of the mountain mass from which it has been carved is considerably more than a mile." Here, in this glacial gorge on the South Fork of the Kings River, Muir had found a rival to his beloved Yosemite Valley, whose own glacial origins still remained to be worked out.

Such a straightforward, factual description hardly hints at the paroxysms of spiritual and esthetic delight that Sierran landscapes so often evoked from this pioneering naturalist and prophet of ecological consciousness. As befits a writer whose influence would grow and crescendo nearly a century after he wrote, Muir ended up exploring himself. Self-exploration remains a worthy motivation for wilderness travel, and Kings Canyon provides an exemplary, if steep, trailhead. Here, "back of beyond" the celebrated realm of giant trees, looms gargantuan southern Sierra wilderness. But be warned: the only way out is up.

Kings Canyon itself has been curiously unnamed by popular usage in recent decades. Today's Cedar Grove, a major focal point for tourism to this park, *is* Kings Canyon.

"Kings Canyon is the upper 8 miles of the gorge, from Lewis Creek at the park boundary up to the confluence of Bubbs Creek and the South Fork of the Kings River," explains William C. Tweed, park management assistant and co-author with Lary M. Dilsaver of the resource history of these parks, *Challenge of the Big Trees.* "That's the way it is listed on the U.S. Geological Survey maps, but park people tend to call the canyon floor up to Roads End 'Cedar Grove.'

"When Kings Canyon National Park was created

33

in 1940 to incorporate General Grant National Park, which was Grant Grove, many people began to confuse the park and the canyon. It seemed easier for park people to refer to Grant Grove and Cedar Grove *in* Kings Canyon National Park. And somewhere along the line many people somehow got the idea that Kings Canyon was *all* of the canyons in the Kings River watershed. It's not that either. It's those 8 miles of canyon for which the park was named.

"To *un*name Kings Canyon," Bill Tweed suggests, would be as unfortunate as "taking the Yosemite Valley out of Yosemite National Park or the Zion Canyon out of Zion National Park."

Kings Canyon's spectacular beauty amply argues that for itself. John Muir's magnum opus on the canyon was his article, "A Rival to the Yosemite," published in Robert Underwood Johnson's *Century Magazine* in November 1891. While writing the article Muir complained to his editor that "My stock of cliff & cascade adjectives are all used up & I am too dull to invent new ones."

He was too modest. Witness the following sentence: "The descent of the Kings River streams is mostly made in the form of cascades, which are outspread in flat plume-like sheets on smooth slopes, or are squeezed in narrow-throated gorges, boiling, seething, in deep swirling pools, pouring from lin [waterfall] to lin, and breaking into ragged, tossing masses of spray and foam in boulder-choked canyons— making marvelous mixtures with the downpouring sunbeams, displaying a thousand forms and colors, and giving forth a great variety of wild mountain melody, which, rolling from side to side against the echoing cliffs, is at length all combined into one smooth, massy sea-like roar."

Spanish explorers who camped along it in 1805 named the Kings River "el rio de los Santos Reyes," River of the Holy Kings. The naming celebrated the day of Epiphany in the Christian church year, traditionally when the Magi or Wise Men arrived in Bethlehem bearing gifts for the newborn Christ Child.

Muir's Kings Canyon article proved an eloquent appeal for expanding the new and then still diminutive Sequoia and General Grant national parks. Muir had traveled to Kings Canyon early in the summer of 1891 with the artist Charles D. Robinson and their guide John Fox. It was not an easy trip, as Muir reported to Underwood in clipped prose: "Had a good trip but a little hard. Had to walk in to the yosemite [the glaciated gorge of Kings Canyon] from the Sequoia Park. Rain, sleet, snow & flooded streams. Slid 2 miles on dead avalanche. Mule with all our grub went down the river but was caught on a grand jam. . . ."

When John Muir writes that the trip was "a little hard," one senses the understatement. By contrast, the article will claim that "Almost anyone able to cross a cobblestoned street in a crowd may climb Mt. Whitney." And Muir will admit that he once spent a November night on Mt. Whitney in snow and intense cold with no blanket or sleeping bag. He had to keep in motion all night to avoid freezing. For the record: Muir rode that dead avalanche by choice not by accident. The practice is not recommended. Muir's solo wilderness habits—he was 53 years old when he took this particular joyride—were not always prophetic of outdoors safety consciousness.

Muir's article in *Century Magazine* led directly to the 1893 withdrawal of the Sierra Forest Reserve from public lands sales. Muir had paid his first visit to the southern Sierra in 1873 as a wanderer. Most of the intervening 20 years he had devoted to becoming a prosperous fruit grower. Now he was returning as an effective, national voice crying for the American wilderness.

With the creation of the Sierra Forest Reserve came the cessation of sales of significant chunks of the wilderness Muir sought to preserve. Forest reserve status did not provide active protection; it meant the lands could no longer be sold to private parties. Unlike parks, forest reserves enjoyed no military protection but were watched over by a very few General Land Office civilians. This was not the park Muir envisioned. However, the battle for a Kings Canyon National Park was now joined.

Importantly, the Sierra Forest Reserve withdrawal marked the end, in the southern Sierra, of the pioneer era and its perception of unlimited resources. To Muir goes most of the credit: "The 'dreamer,'" Robert Underwood Johnson wrote of him, "proved to be a propagandist of the most practical sort." Now the task was to begin questioning the exploitative mentality.

Scottish-born John Muir first explored the southern Sierra in 1873 to study its geology and the Big Trees. He marveled at Kings Canyon's glacial history and named Giant Forest. In the 1890s he championed creation of one grand southern Sierra national park whose extent is now approached by Sequoia and Kings Canyon National Parks. Muir founded the Sierra Club to promote conservation causes and served as its president for many years.

Cross Section of the Sierra Nevada

At Ash Mountain headquarters for Sequoia and Kings Canyon National Parks the elevation is 1,700 feet above sea level. To the east, park elevations top out at 14,494 feet on Mt. Whitney, highest point in the contiguous United States. Stupendous canyons deeply incise high peaks: Kern Canyon, in southern Sequoia National Park, is 6,000 feet deep; many canyons exceed 4,000 feet in depth. Glaciers gouged some; streams carved others. Just outside Kings Canyon National Park, the Kings River Canyon reaches a depth of 8,200 feet measured from river level to Spanish Mountain's summit. There the canyon is without peer in this country—deeper than the Snake River's Hells Canyon in Idaho, and the Colorado River's Grand Canyon in Arizona. The Generals Highway and Kings Canyon Highway weave their ways into the parks through canyons. At Roads End in Kings Canyon, granite walls rise nearly a mile above river level on the flat valley floor. The cross section of the Sierra Nevada illustrated below runs from the North Fork of the Kaweah River on the west, through the Giant Forest, to Mt. Whitney on the east. The straight-line distance represented is 34 miles. In the Sierra's western foothills, dry, hot summers give rise to the drought-resistant plant community known as chaparral and to scattered blue oak woodlands. The giant sequoia groves occur on the Sierra's west slopes, mostly between 5,000 and 7,000 feet in elevation. Average annual precipitation runs high here; at Giant Forest, elevation 6,500 feet, the figure is 44 inches.

Foothills *feature the tough, drought-resistant chaparral plant community and the threatened blue oak woodlands. Foothills chaparral ranges from 1,000 to nearly 5,000 feet in elevation.*

Giant sequoia trees *reproduce naturally only on the Sierra Nevada's west slope. Sequoias grow in 75 groves generally found at elevations between 5,000 and 7,000 feet.*

North Fork Kaweah River

Marble Fork Kaweah River

GIANT FOREST

Moro Rock
6725ft

Moving from west to east in this cross-section, the distance from the North Fork of the Kaweah River to Mount Whitney is approximately 34 mil

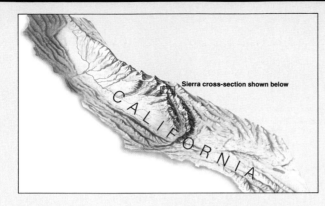

Sierra cross-section shown below

CALIFORNIA

Parts of a Larger Whole

Today's parks are not self-contained ecological units but parts of larger ecosystems. They are subject to air pollution, acid rain, ozone damage to plant life, and other problems originating outside their boundaries. Saving giant sequoia trees is no mere matter of drawing boundaries around them. Saving them now requires a larger social vision of environmental conscience.

Deep canyons, *both stream-cut and gouged by glaciers, are incised into the Sierra Nevada. Near the parks at Spanish Mountain, the Kings River Canyon is North America's deepest.*

Mt. Whitney *rises to 14,494 feet above sea level. The parks boast eight mountain divides separating major river systems—and assuring rugged backcountry.*

Kern Canyon

Triple
Divide Peak
12634ft

Mount Whitney
14494ft

Foothills Life: Chaparral and Oak Woodlands

The foothills of Sequoia and Kings Canyon National Parks become increasingly significant as similar lands outside the parks fall prey to heavy grazing and residential development. **Chaparral** formerly covered 8.5 percent of California. However, development has obliterated much of it. These parks protect important remnants of this mediterranean ecosystem, a thick elfin forest of bushes standing 3 to 8 feet tall. Chaparral ranges in elevation from 1,000 to 5,000 feet. Chamise is its most character-istic plant in much of the area. Important to many wildlife species, berries of the manzanita bush feed bears, deer, birds, and rodents. Spring shows of blooming shrubs are glorious; in years following fire these are replaced by fields of wildflowers. **Blue oak woodlands** occur between 500 and 2,500 feet in elevation. Blue oaks are named for their leathery leaves, blue-green above and paler below. Parklands protect these trees from the damage by grazing, land clearing, and wood-cutting that is reducing their numbers elsewhere. High in protein, acorns are important wildlife food, particularly as bears and deer fatten for the coming rigors of winter. Indians of this area preferred acorns of the black oak as a food crop. **Black oaks** grow between 3,500 and 7,500 feet in elevation.

1 Manzanita
2 Brown towhee
3 Red-tailed hawk
4 Lark sparrow
5 Coyote
6 California buckeye
7 Southern alligator lizard
8 California quail
9 Scrub jay
10 Chamise
11 Redbud
12 Yucca
13 Western fence lizard
14 Turkey vulture
15 Blue oak
16 Mule deer
17 Harlequin lupine
18 Gray fox
19 California ground squirrel
20 Black bear
21 Acorn woodpecker
22 Western rattlesnake
23 Poison oak

Flowers Patiently Await Fire

Chaparral vegetation co-evolved with fire; it burns quickly, but many seeds survive. Resinous shrubs may explode into flame. Burrows suffice to protect some small mammals as fire sweeps past. Wildflowers burst on the scene for 3 to 4 years after a burn. Seeds of tall-stalked, yellow-flowering *Dicentra*, or golden ear drops, may wait 70 years for post-fire conditions to allow them to germinate.

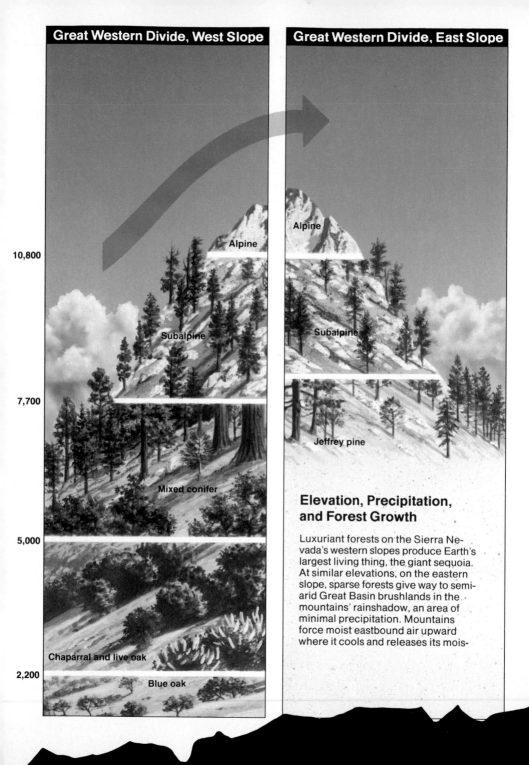

Alpine

Alpine

10,800

Subalpine

Subalpine

7,700

Jeffrey pine

Mixed conifer

Elevation, Precipitation, and Forest Growth

Luxuriant forests on the Sierra Nevada's western slopes produce Earth's largest living thing, the giant sequoia. At similar elevations, on the eastern slope, sparse forests give way to semi-arid Great Basin brushlands in the mountains' rainshadow, an area of minimal precipitation. Mountains force moist eastbound air upward where it cools and releases its mois-

5,000

Chaparral and live oak

2,200

Blue oak

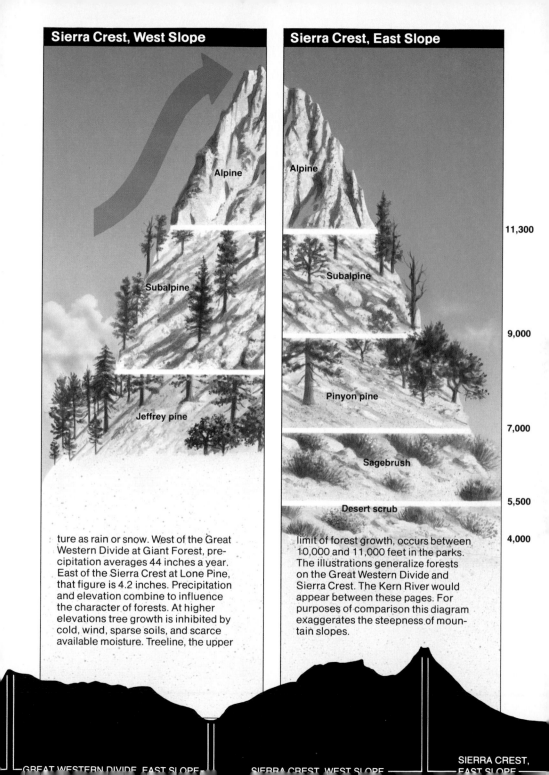

Sierra Crest, West Slope

Alpine

Subalpine

Jeffrey pine

Sierra Crest, East Slope

Alpine

Subalpine

Pinyon pine

Sagebrush

Desert scrub

11,300

9,000

7,000

5,500

4,000

ture as rain or snow. West of the Great Western Divide at Giant Forest, precipitation averages 44 inches a year. East of the Sierra Crest at Lone Pine, that figure is 4.2 inches. Precipitation and elevation combine to influence the character of forests. At higher elevations tree growth is inhibited by cold, wind, sparse soils, and scarce available moisture. Treeline, the upper

limit of forest growth, occurs between 10,000 and 11,000 feet in the parks. The illustrations generalize forests on the Great Western Divide and Sierra Crest. The Kern River would appear between these pages. For purposes of comparison this diagram exaggerates the steepness of mountain slopes.

GREAT WESTERN DIVIDE, EAST SLOPE

SIERRA CREST, WEST SLOPE

SIERRA CREST, EAST SLOPE

Ponderosa pine

Height to 200 feet
Elevation range:
3,500 to 6,500 feet

Sugar pine

Height to 210 feet
Elevation range:
5,000 to 7,500 feet

Red fir

Foxtail pine

Height to 75 feet
Elevation range:
9,500 to 11,500 feet

Height to 180 feet
Elevation range:
7,000 to 9,500 feet

The world's largest living things are thought to be named in honor of the Cherokee Indian, Se-quo-yah, who devised a remarkably effective alphabet for his people. Within just a few years of its promulgation, most Cherokees had achieved literacy in their native language.

Three major rivers arise in these parks, all beginning with the letter K: Kings, Kaweah, and Kern. Like couriers they carry Pacific Ocean moisture back toward sea level. The rivers' waters begin largely as snowfall—forced out of eastbound clouds as they rise in attempting to crest and cross the Sierra. The Kings River mostly irrigates the Nation's richest agricultural district in southern Fresno County. The Kaweah River irrigates a prolific portion of Tulare County. The Kern irrigates Kern County, also known as "the salad bowl of America" for the prodigious quantities of vegetables grown there. Much of central California's renowned agricultural productivity depends on these rivers arising in Sequoia and Kings Canyon National Parks.

Despite their enthusiasm and boisterousness, these three rivers generally do not reach the ocean today. The Kings and Kaweah flow into the Tulare Basin. Before agricultural use diverted its tributary waters, the two rivers flowed into vast, shallow, and marsh-fringed Tulare Lake. Tulare Lake is now dry except briefly in periods of heavy runoff.

Although the Kern is 155 miles long, 80 percent of its water originates as melting snow within its first 15 miles. The Kern is unusual also in that, of all west slope Sierran streams, it flows not west but due south for some 70 miles before heading westward into the southern San Joaquin Valley. So rough-and-tumble is the Kern that a nickname is the Kern-trary. On shaded relief maps, its canyon marks a long and barely sinuous glacial gouge contrasting sharply with its flanking jumbled terrain.

Writing of the Kern River, so rambunctious in Sequoia National Park, Vivienne L. George notes that ". . . when the waters reach the valley floor they are absorbed by the desert sand, and the stream ambles along, sluggishly as if it were panting in the heat." Today the Kern River comes to rest in human-created Lake Buena Vista. From 1880 to 1888, writes George, ". . . the waters of the Kern were the object of a violent and bloody range war waged both in the field and in the courts." There was not enough water to support the development schemes of both parties. A legal compromise ended the war and "paved the way for creation of the massive Kern County Land Company, one of the West's largest cattle ranching-truck farming-oil producing operations."

It was only 102 years before the Kern's discovery by non-Indians in 1776 that a Frenchman had proved that precipitation alone fed stream flow. Water was not bubbling up, as previously thought, from deep within the Earth. John Muir merely extended a metaphor when he called the Sierra Nevada a fountain of life. By the late 19th century the idea that streams originate with precipitation was well entrenched in the minds of hydroelectric engineers and irrigationists. You can see their effects near Sequoia National Park's Ash Mountain Entrance and in the boundary history of Kings Canyon National Park.

Beginning in 1898, the Kaweah hydroelectric system was developed over 20 years, first by the Mount Whitney Power Company. The system's Powerhouse 3 lies just outside Sequoia National Park near Ash Mountain. Flumes completed in 1913 bring water to the powerhouse from the Middle and Marble forks of the Kaweah River.

Because of hydroelectric plans for the Kings River watershed, parts of Tehipite Valley and Kings Canyon had been excluded from Kings Canyon National Park upon its creation in 1940. Not until 1965 were boundaries redrawn to include all of them. Inundation of these magnificent glacial gorges would have been a tragedy on the order of the damming of Hetch Hetchy Valley early this century within Yosemite National Park. However, in 1948 the City of Los Angeles filed with California's State Water Board and the Federal Power Commission to build dams and power stations in both canyons. The city also sought similar developments at several other sites in Kings Canyon National Park. Local water interests opposed the projects, fearing loss of control over the water with no local benefits. Local interests also fought water development on the North Fork of the Kings River. The water would become part of the federal Central Valley Project—and again some water would have gone to Los Angeles. These issues were not settled until 1963, and the canyons were included in the park two years later. Kings Canyon National Park embraced its namesake at last. John Muir's "one great national park" was nearing fruition now in two national parks.

Kings Canyon National Park was created in 1940 primarily to protect its wilderness. The 60 years of

Cattleman Hale Tharp settled in Giant Forest, where his cabin addition in a hollowed sequoia log may be seen. **Bottom:** *Army Capt. Charles Young served as acting superintendent of Sequoia National Park in 1903.*

Winter snowpack in the Sierra Nevada provides magnificent natural water storage on which much of California's agricultural wealth depends. Its runoff also generates electrical power. When Col. George Stewart mustered forces to save the giant sequoias, scenery was only one issue. San Joaquin Valley agriculture used water husbanded by the mountains' mantle of forests. Snowfields, forests, lakes, and streams collect, store, and release the bounty of the wet winters throughout the dry summers. The amount of water stored as snowpack continues to increase through mid-April at higher elevations. Meltoff begins in April and continues heavy through May in average years. October is the month in which the least water runs out of the park. In years of low snowpack accumulation, bears range wider distances for food. Rodent populations drop, affecting many predators. The Kings River formerly drained into Tulare Lake, with water flowing through the San Joaquin River to San Francisco Bay in years of high runoff. Consumed by irrigation, the water no longer reaches the ocean. The Kern and Kaweah rivers, formerly draining into basins and not the sea, are also taken up by agriculture now.

Snowpack and Agriculture

If California were a nation it would be the world's seventh largest agricultural producer. Many of its orchards, grains, and row crops depend on irrigation waters originating as snowpack in the Sierra Nevada. Except in the foothills, most of the parks' annual average precipitation falls from October through May as snow. Snowpack holds the moisture until summer reaches higher elevations. By then crops are up and growing in the already hot and dry San Joaquin Valley.

Measuring Snowpack

The slow release of water from snowpack creates a critical difference between the seasons of the heavens and the rivers' seasons. Water from winter storms becomes available into the summer months. Californians eagerly await news of the year's snowpack. Shortfalls may mean restricted water use on farms and ranches and in homes. Rangers ski cross-country to record snowpack accumulations at survey sites throughout the parks.

Global Climate Change

Global climate change caused by human activities could place great stress on life as we know it, with potentially serious implications for Sierran parks. Pushing the snowline higher up mountains, increasing temperature, and/or decreasing precipitation, for example, could be expected to lessen water storage, alter species and habitat distribution, and make fire more frequent and severe. Species at high elevations or at the southern margin of their range might not survive. With their extremely limited range, the distribution of giant sequoias might even be affected.

SIERRA

OWENS VALLEY

Fresno

Middle Fork

Mount Whitney

Kings River

Visalia

NEVADA

JOAQUIN

Kaweah River

Lake Kaweah

Tule R.

Tulare Lake bed

VALLEY

Lake Isabella

Kern River

Buena Vista Lake bed

RANGES

TEHACHAPI MOUNTAINS

• Los Angeles

Life in Lakes and Ponds . . . Before Trout Were Introduced

The parks contain some 2,650 lakes and ponds, and their well-meaning manipulation over more than a century has left a legacy of artificial aquatic habitats. Fish planting begun in the 1870s created streams and lakes with non-native fish, particularly European brown and eastern brook trout, as shown in the right side of the illustration. On the west side of the parks, rainbow trout were native. On the south side of Sequoia National Park, there were native golden trout, California's state fish. Most rain-

bow and golden trout present today originated in hatcheries or are hybrids. After the Ice Ages, thousands of glacial lakes were left without fish, and they developed populations of insects and freshwater crustaceans, as shown on the left page. Fish planting disrupted these natural aquatic systems, as the introduced trout ate most of the larger invertebrates and tadpoles of the mountain yellow-legged frog. Scientists speculate that the decline of waterbirds in high-elevation lakes may reflect this loss of invertebrate

fauna. Various competitive bait organisms and non-native plants also were introduced. For example, elodea plants used in many home aquariums now carpet the bottoms of some of the Rae Lakes. In many waters that supported native trout populations, introduced fish supplanted native species, as shown on the right page. To help restore natural conditions in lakes and streams, the National Park Service no longer stocks fish. Note: one lake rarely contains all the trout species shown.

... And After

1 Isoetes
2 Mountain yellow-legged frog
3 Jeffrey's shooting star
4 Carex
5 Alder fly adult
6 Predaceous diving beetle larva
7 Leech
8 Midge larva (Chironomidae)
9 Mayfly nymph
10 Clam (Pisidium)
11 Amphipod
12 Fairy shrimp
13 Sponge
14 Tadpole
15 Marsh marigold
16 Copepod
17 Rotifer (Conochilus)
18 Water flea
19 Alder fly larva
20 Predaceous diving beetle
21 Mayfly adult

22 Spotted sandpiper
23 Golden trout
24 Elodea
25 Brook trout
26 Water mite (Hydracarina)
27 Invertebrates
28 Damselfly nymph
29 Rainbow trout

The Frog That Disappeared

Sometime in the 1970s the foothill yellow-legged frog disappeared. Various amphibians have similarly disappeared, from California to Eurasia. Nobody knows why; speculation involves pollution and global-scale climatic change. That a formerly abundant frog has apparently disappeared from protected national parks leaves scientists apprehensive.

controversy over southern Sierra resource values since the creation of Sequoia National Park had bought time for wilderness recreation proponents. Heirs of utilitarianism lost out to heirs of John Muir, who had noted: "The tendency nowadays to wander in the wildernesses is delightful to see. Thousands of tired, nerve-shaken, over-civilized people are beginning to find out that going to the mountains is going home; that wildness is a necessity; and that mountain parks and reservations are useful not only as fountains of timber and irrigating rivers, but as fountains of life."

Even Muir's heirs had not caught up with his vision of wilderness "fountains of life." The widening and then deepening ecological vision just now penetrating American lifestyles would be required. To value wilderness for human recreation is to miss, even among its spiritual values for humans, its intrinsic values. Intrinsic values include how wilderness, not just a place but a quality of natural processes, helps perpetuate the variety of life forms, the ecological roles they play, and the genetic information they preserve.

Your travels in these parks—from foothills chaparral, to giant forests, and perhaps afoot to mountain heights—reveal extensive vegetative diversity. There are more than 1,290 native herbs, trees, and shrubs in the parks, with new species discovered yearly. The extreme changes in elevation offer multitudes of habitat niches. Equally important ecological niches exist in time, as when, for example, after a fire in chaparral the habitat niches are far different than before the fire. The National Park Service strives to preserve the *processes* that created these parks' richness over time. Created as a wilderness park before its time, Kings Canyon achieved official wilderness designation for much of its extent 44 years later. Both acts transcended utilitarianism. By preserving diversity in the southern Sierra, both also transcended merely human visions of the values underlying national parks.

The red-brown bark of the sturdy manzanita bears such a high sheen that it sometimes looks wet when its foothills chaparral habitat is decidedly dry. A yucca plant fans out in the foreground. Chaparral, a vegetation type found in mediterranean climates, depends on periodic wildfire to maintain its vigorous diversity.

Restoring Native Bighorns

Native bighorn sheep were common in eastern California mountains until the mid-19th century. Then, domestic sheep were herded into this native's domain. Domestic sheep—John Muir called them "hoofed locusts"—denuded Sierra forage and introduced diseases to which native bighorns had little resistance. Hunting increased in the late 19th century, and bighorn populations were sharply reduced to mere remnants confined to remote southern Sierra fastnesses. By the 1970s extinction threatened. Fortunately, two natural herds survived along the eastern boundary of Sequoia and Kings Canyon National Parks. In the 1970s, concern for their continued health led to a cooperative effort by the National Park Service, Forest Service, and California Department of Fish and Game to restore bighorns to other parts of their historical range. In 1979 bighorns from the Baxter herd were reintroduced near Mt. Langley in Sequoia National Park's southeastern corner. With later additions this herd has survived. In 1986 the nonprofit Goldman Fund made it possible to reintroduce bighorns—also from the Baxter herd—just east of Yosemite National Park. Presently only the Baxter herd produces enough surplus sheep for relocation. Further reintroductions will follow as sheep numbers allow—about 30 are needed to start a new herd. Reintroductions protect the sheep by expanding their range and, potentially, increasing their overall numbers. However, since all these reintroduced sheep winter near domestic sheep, they are at peril from disease, their worst enemy. The next planned reintroduction is to the Great Western Divide in Sequoia National Park. This will estab-

lish a herd isolated within the parks from domestic sheep and disease. Male and female bighorns bear horns: the ram's are coiled; the ewe's are curved. During rutting season, competing rams fight by charging each other, crashing head on. This intense, full-tilt running and butting of horns inflicts no apparent damage to either party, but it can be heard up to a half-mile away! Individual battles may last for two hours before the rams quit. Sometimes free-for-alls

break out as several rams get into the act, certainly an astounding event to witness. In early May, six months after these theatrics, lambs are born, usually one to a ewe, rarely twins. The white lambs generally darken to the drab, gray-brown adult pelage as they mature. Drab coats make bighorns difficult to spot even if one gains access to their rugged highcountry domain.

Mystery of Four Furbearers

"These animals are almost too rare to study," says research biologist Dave Graber. He speaks of the Sierra Nevada red fox, wolverine, and fisher. Except for the fisher, these and the marten are boreal creatures adapted to northern latitudes. As the Ice Ages ended, only high mountains provided habitat for them this far south. Here the wolverine, fox, and fisher are at the extreme southern limits of their ranges. The marten is nearly so. "They barely hang on here," says Graber, "and then only because of the elevation." A clear danger of global warming is that its effects would counteract those of elevation. "Global warming could push these furbearers off the tops of the mountains, in effect," Graber emphasizes. These creatures are wilderness denizens associated with undisturbed, uncut habitat. Fishers, for example, are associated with uncut ponderosa pine forest. These parks provide valuable refuge; they are surrounded by forest lands subject to logging, grazing, second-home building, and other forms of development. Fifty years ago habitats inside and outside the park were largely the same.

Trapper Shorty Lovelace

Joseph Walter "Shorty" Lovelace (1886-1963) trapped throughout Kings Canyon country for more than 20 years until the park's creation in 1940. He mainly sought, in order of pelt value, fisher, wolverine, and marten. What impact Shorty had on today's reduced numbers is not known. Only martens were abundant even in Shorty's day.

3

1 Wolverine
2 Red fox
3 Marten
4 Fisher

4

Bears

A rancher shot California's last authenticated grizzly bear in 1922 just outside today's Kings Canyon National Park. However, workers in Sequoia National Park reported seeing a grizzly in 1924. Since then black bears, much smaller than grizzlies, have been largely without enemies other than humans. Black bears, whose colors range from light brown through black, are omnivores, eating both plants and animals. They have crushing molars—not unlike yours—rather than the cutting molars of carnivorous cats, for example. Opportunistic feeders, Sierran black bears eat berries, herbs, grasses, acorns, insects (ants and yellow jackets), occasional ground-nesting birds, and deer fawns and will scavenge carrion. Black bears' home ranges cover 4 to 10 square miles and are relatively stable. In the fall bears often move to lower elevations to feed on nutritious acorns. In winter they den in cavities of tree roots, among rocks, or in fallen logs and the bases of hollow trees. In mild winters some bears do not den. At birth black bear cubs hardly fulfill their romanticized image as arch predators. Born in the den in late January, cubs weigh just 12 to 16 ounces and measure 8 inches long. For 40 days they will be blind. At two weeks old they will weigh 2 pounds, doubling that by the end of five weeks. Bear milk is high in protein; with a fat content of 25 to 33 percent, it fosters rapid weight gain. Cubs, usually two in a litter, generally stay with their mother for about 15 months when food is plentiful. She gives birth only every other year because she can care for only one set of young at a time. Her accumulated fat helps manufacture her cubs' milk during their hibernation fast. Black bears can live to be 12 or 15 years old, sometimes 20. In the oak forest and mixed conifer forest, bear population density is about one per square mile, much less at higher elevations. The major threat to park bears is habituation to human food sources—a one-way road to the necessity of a bear's destruction.

Under New Management
The National Park Service pursues a rigorous human-bear management program. Its purpose is to restore the natural distribution and behavior of bears and to prevent personal injuries and property damage. The chief strategy is to separate bears from human food sources. Proper food storage is required by law in the parks at all times, and regulations are strictly enforced. Do your part to prevent a black bear's untimely death. Keep a clean camp, store food properly, deposit all garbage in bear-proof cans or dumpsters, and scare away bears that approach you.

Profiles of black bear (top) and grizzly bear

Paw print, black bear

Paw print, grizzly bear

Wildlife

Yellow-bellied marmot

Dragonfly

Mule deer

Gray fox

Great horned owl

Mountain chickadee

Red-winged blackbird

Northern oriole

Black bear

Coyote

Young bighorn sheep

Mountain lions

Western tanager

Hermit thrush

California thrasher

Mountain yellow-legged frog

The Big Trees:
What Is Natural?

The General Sherman Tree in Giant Forest is the world's largest living thing. It weighs nearly 1,400 tons, and one branch measures nearly 7 feet in diameter. This giant sequoia probably began growing sometime between 300 and 700 B.C. Four of the world's five largest trees stand in Giant Forest.

Fearful that even the General Grant Tree would be toppled and turned into grape stakes, the U.S. Surveyor General for California unilaterally withdrew Grant Grove from further homesteading in 1880. Fortunately, the General Land Office in Washington, D.C., upheld his independent action. For a decade Grant Grove would remain a four-square-mile forested ark in a sea of private logging lands.

In another fortuitous action, a newspaper editor in nearby Visalia late in 1885 forestalled probable destruction of the Giant Forest, the Big Tree grove first settled by cattleman Hale Tharp and named by John Muir. Timber barons were not at issue. Instead, it was a group of labor union socialists devising a Utopian community, the Kaweah Colony, who had chosen timbering for its economic life. They filed land claims embracing the Giant Forest, which required that they publish a legal notice in the *Visalia Delta* newspaper. A proofreader notified editor George Stewart that most claimants gave the same San Francisco address. Suspecting a timber swindle, Stewart asked the government to investigate.

The Kaweah Colony probably acted within its rights under public land laws. However, after much controversy, the government asserted ownership of the Giant Forest. Nonetheless, the grove was not included in Sequoia National Park as first established in 1890. Congress would significantly enlarge the park one week later to include Giant Forest. By then colonists had forged a haul road nearly into the grove. In an editorial Stewart said the government should make a payment to those who built the road, but it never did. The colony's road was destined to carry not lumber but national park visitors.

Col. George W. Stewart had been born in 1857 near Placerville, California. At age 19 he began writing for the *Delta* and became its local editor in 1878 at age 21. Except for a brief absence, Stewart edited the *Delta* until 1899. Stewart was a respected

What is the difference between sequoias and redwoods?

The giant sequoia, **below,** *has a column-like trunk over 30 feet in diameter; huge, stout branches; its bark is cinnamon-colored; and the tree reproduces from seed only. Its scientific name is* Sequoiadendron giganteum. *It is sometimes called the Sierra redwood.*

journalist who also was published widely in both nonfiction and poetry. He retired from the California National Guard (1887-1903) as a lieutenant colonel.

"The story of the founding of Sequoia National Park, when it comes to be fully told, will stand proudly in the annals of America with that of the founding of Yellowstone," historian Francis P. Farquhar wrote. "In the files of the *Visalia Delta* will be found much of the material for that story, for it was as editor of that paper that George Stewart conducted the campaign."

Stewart and his associates, knowing the land, land surveys, and public land laws, repeatedly headed off development. He was so modest and self-effacing that the full extent of his role in the creation of Sequoia National Park will never be known. In ceremonies in Visalia in 1929, Stewart was acclaimed as the park's founder and, as Farquhar says, "the savior of the big trees of Giant Forest." That day it was announced that a peak on the Great Western Divide had been named Mount Stewart in his honor.

One who extolled Stewart's work that day was Col. John Roberts White, the park's second civilian superintendent, from 1920 to 1938, and its fourth superintendent, from 1941 to 1947. Except for Stewart's work, White declared, "we might now be sitting upon a stump of a blackened wilderness instead of enjoying the full benefits not only of beauty but of water for your summer crops. Give to Col. Stewart the entire credit, for it was he who did it. . . ."

White's remarks about both beauty and water recognized the tactics Stewart and friends used to save the Big Trees. In November 1889, supporters convened representatives of Fresno, Tulare, Kern, and Merced counties to petition Congress "to protect all the timbers covering the water-sheds embraced within the unoccupied public Domain of the State of California." Giant sequoias were not mentioned. Irrigation, the raisin industry, and "the developing of a wealth of resources equal to that of Egypt in the days of the Pharaohs" *were* mentioned.

Stewart was a pragmatist with close ties to his political alliance of farmers, growers, and tourism boosters. In lesser known aspects of Stewart's life work—his poetry, Sierran nature studies, and work with Yokuts Indians—one finds the measure of this man's soulful veneration of the giant sequoias.

If Colonel Stewart founded Sequoia National Park, his eulogizer, Col. John Roberts White, shaped its appeal to visitors right to our day. If Stewart saved the Giant Forest *for* posterity, the Oxford-educated White designed actions to save it *from* posterity. The parks' present managers hope to complete White's grand design soon.

In a young National Park Service, John Roberts White, 50 years ahead of his time, intuited basic tenets of managing parks to protect natural values. His ideas sometimes rankled and frustrated first National Park Service Director Stephen T. Mather and his development-oriented successor, Horace M. Albright. White's ideas also irked concession operators. White relished his role in preventing overdevelopment: he once said his epitaph should read: "He was an obstructionist in Sequoia National Park. . . ." As William Tweed notes, Colonel White "probably looks better to the National Park Service today than he did to his contemporaries."

Automobiles had already shaped park visitors' experiences when White took charge of Sequoia and General Grant national parks in 1920. Their straight-line boundaries did not take natural features into account, and Sequoia National Park was less than half its present size. Its major enlargement eastward to Mt. Whitney and the Sierra crest would take place in 1926. Then White would be even less content to watch people visit the park only from cars. He decided to confine development to the park's western portion. He had park maps printed that said:

"This map is placed in your hands with a definite object in view—to encourage you to leave your automobile and *walk*. Through the Giant Forest run many miles of safe and easy trails. . . . You are now entering the greatest forest in the world, containing 3,000 trees more than 10 feet in diameter. Don't leave until you have seen it and this you cannot do from an automobile."

White's major management legacy—that present park managers hope to complete soon—was to begin to remove park development from Giant Forest. "We should boldly ask ourselves," White told a 1936 meeting of park superintendents, "whether we want the national parks to duplicate the features and entertainments of other resorts, or whether we want them to stand for something distinct, and we hope

Taller and usually only 8 to 10 feet in diameter, the coast redwood has a more usual conifer profile and branch structure. It reproduces by seed and root sprouts. Its common name comes from the color of its heartwood, not its gray bark. Its scientific name is Sequoia sempervirens. *A third species, the dawn redwood, is indigenous to China. Its scientific name is* Metasequoia glyptostroboides.

"I never saw a Big Tree that had died a natural death," John Muir wrote of the giant sequoia, "barring accidents they seem to be immortal, being exempt from all the diseases that afflict and kill other trees. Unless destroyed by man, they live on indefinitely until burned, smashed by lightning, or cast down by storms, or by the giving way of the ground on which they stand." Muir's observation remains generally accurate. The life story of the giant sequoia begins with a plethora of small seeds—91,000 sequoia seeds weigh just 1 pound. Unlike its cousin the coast redwood, which can sprout from root and stump,

Seed, Cone, and Bark

Giant sequoias sprout only from seeds so small and light they look like oat flakes. Mature trees produce yearly crops of up to 2,000 cones about the size of hens' eggs and may hold 40,000 cones bearing half a million seeds. Sequoia bark, up to 18 inches thick, prevents trees' being damaged by most fires. High tannin content provides the tree protection against insect damage and heartrot, protection critical to longevity.

Cone ready to disperse seeds

Cambium layer
Heartwood
Bark

Fire scar
Sapwood

Mature seed   Germinating seed   Sheds seed coat   At 2 weeks

the sequoia can sprout only from seed. To germinate and survive, sequoia seeds must fall on bare, mineral soil. All seeds fall out of cones eventually, but they accomplish nothing unless soil conditions are right. Fires bring down large numbers of seeds on top of soil burned clear of duff.

Foraging by Douglas squirrels —or chickarees—sees multitudes of cones harvested and thousands of seeds released. In the absence of fire, however, these seeds rarely fall on suitable seedbed. Larvae of a tiny cone-boring beetle also cause the release of sequoia seeds, but their fate remains fruitless as well in the

absence of recent fire. The sequoia seed must fall on bare mineral soil, not on duff. Fires not only bare the soil but also burn off competing trees such as shade-tolerant white firs.

Range

Giant sequoias grow naturally only on the western slopes of California's Sierra Nevada, mostly between 5,000 and 7,000 feet in elevation.

There are about 75 groves. Ancestors of these trees ranged more widely when moist climate conditions favored their growth.

After a fire many seedlings sprout immediately under the parent tree. A Douglas squirrel (right) chews on a sequoia cone.

General Grant Our National Christmas Tree and a living monument to all U.S. war dead is the General Grant Tree, third largest in the world. Congress made it a National Shrine in 1956. Annual Christmas services are held at the tree. Height: 267.4 feet. Estimated age: 2,000 years.

California Struck by lightning in 1967, the California tree lost 25 feet of top. To put out the fire smoldering in its top, a park forester climbed a nearby tree and, crossing a rope between them, extinguished it from above with a hose. Height: 255 feet. Age: unestimated.

Ed by Ned Twin trees at Round Meadow were named in 1906 with signs made by the Jordan family camped there. With a hot iron the family burned "Ed" into one little sign and "By Ned" into another. The trees were named for John Jordan and Ed Fudge. Height: unmeasured. Age: unestimated.

No name Located in Giant Forest Village, this Big Tree has no name. It measures 17 feet dbh (in diameter at breast height). The parks abandoned the practice of naming the Big Trees after World War II. Height: unmeasured. Age: unestimated.

Role of Fire in Sequoia Groves

Toward summer's end in the dry season forest conditions favor fire, and lightning storms are not uncommon in the mountains. Fire scars in tree rings dating back 2,000 years show that fires have occurred naturally at varying intervals, generally between three and 35 years, in sequoia forests. Giant sequoias are adapted to periodic fire. They even take advantage of fire to gain a competitive edge for reproduction. Under natural fire conditions sequoia bark usually protects the trees against significant damage. At up to 18 inches thick and extremely fibrous, sequoia bark not only resists burning but also insulates the tree against fire's heat. Should fire penetrate the bark and scar the cambium, new growth—one-half inch of new wood and bark can be added per year—can heal the scar. Eventually the scar may be completely covered and the tree protected anew against subsequent fire.

Fire also prepares the bare, mineral soil required by sequoia seeds for germination. It burns off undergrowth and trees that compete for the abundant sunlight young sequoias require. The sequoia's cone-and-seed strategy certainly evolved with fire. Sequoia cones retain their seeds —unlike other trees in their forest environs—in closed cones for perhaps 20 years. When fire burns through the forest the hot air dries out

older cones. They open up and, within one to two weeks, begin to rain down their seed loads onto the fire-swept, bare soil. The reproductive success of giant sequoias demands only that each tree produce just one maturing offspring over its lifespan of several thousand years. The inset photo shows a researcher studying fire's effects as part of the effort to help restore natural conditions to the giant sequoia groves.

Perhaps no two figures influenced Sequoia National Park more than Col. John Roberts White, left, and Col. George Stewart. From nearby Visalia, newspaperman Stewart orchestrated the campaign leading to the park's creation in 1890. White served as the park's second and fourth civilian superintendents. He blocked inappropriate facilities and entertainments in the new park and oversaw construction of ecologically sensitive backcountry trails.

better in our national life." He wanted development plans "subordinated to that atmosphere which though unseen, is no less surely felt by all who visit those eternal masterpieces. . . ."

"This is an odd national park in that most of the old buildings are about to disappear," says Bill Tweed. "In a few years the *human* Giant Forest will be gone. This park is involved in an unprecedented campaign to obliterate its traditional built environment—the traditional public perception of a national park."

When White came on duty in 1920, park policy permitted people to build cabins up to 12x14 feet with canvas additions right in Giant Forest. Canvas additions "sometimes sprawled over half an acre," White's wife, Fay, once said. It took 13 years to evict all these park residents. White also fenced Big Trees to protect them from car bumpers and souvenir hunters' hatchets and their shallow root systems from soil compaction.

Largely unsuccessful in clearing buildings from Giant Forest, White did limit the number of accommodations offered by concessioners there. He also resisted upscale resort hotels such as those at Yellowstone, Grand Canyon, and Yosemite; park lodgings should take second place to the Big Trees. White reduced campsite numbers in Giant Forest. Over the years he prevented intrusions of a miniature golf course, pony rides, movie theaters, dance halls, hay rides, cable lifts, and many other amusements.

White proved equally sensitive in backcountry management, developing trail systems and camping and stock facilities. Built between 1927 and 1932, the High Sierra Trail was for White the "finest of Sierra trails." Stretching from Giant Forest to Mt. Whitney's summit, the trail has introduced thousands of hikers to grand mountain terrain. White helped select the route and insisted on skirting fragile alpine areas. Necessary improvements would be simple and built of native materials. Road access would be minimal. Writing in the *Journal of Forest History*, Rick Hydrick notes: "White's farsighted program for backcountry use was remarkable in an age of few standards, limited budgets, incomplete utilization, and much environmental abuse." White said backcountry travel was "the best accommodation in the park."

"White's knowledge of the Big Trees and the

park's broader natural history exceeded . . . romantic inclinations," Hydrick writes. "Indeed, he often anticipated modern ecological themes. His first book, *Big Trees* . . . was a major effort at scientific interpretation and is still widely read by students of Sierra Nevada natural history."

One wonder of giant sequoias that Colonel White often imparted to visitors at his weekly campfire program was their uncanny resilience in the face of fire. Unfortunately, for decades, forest fires started by lightning had been put out whenever possible. Were we not mandated to protect the Big Trees? The resounding answer was yes, but few people realized that suppression of natural fires was not saving giant sequoias. It was, in fact, hampering their reproduction. Like building hotels in sequoia groves, the early management decision to suppress fire has now become one of the parks' current problems.

"One of the parks' major goals is to restore the natural effects of fire to the ecosystem in a safe manner," says fire management expert Tom Nichols while showing a visitor a prescribed burn site in Giant Forest. A big problem, Nichols explains, is public relations and, specifically, blackened trees.

"Some people don't want to see trees with blackened bark. Yet there have always been sequoias with blackened bark. What a sequoia tree or grove looks like is a moving target over time. On the one day that you visit the parks, you may wish they didn't have blackened bark. They should look like the beautiful photographs. Well, no one publishes beautiful pictures of blackened trees."

The fire that causes it is essential to sequoia growth and reproduction. "The black begins to wash off almost immediately. In a few years it will be barely noticeable." Nichols points at a giant sequoia: "Look below those irregularities in the bark profile. See the little black spots? They occur where rain can't wash down the bark. You can see these black spots on many Big Trees, the signs of ancient fires. All mature sequoias have probably had blackened bark in the past. That's the way they live." And as far as we know, they always have. Giant sequoias evolved with fire.

Fire may even account for the height of giant sequoias as it does for their seed and reproductive

Development That Didn't Happen

Sequoia and Kings Canyon National Parks are significant in part for their contrast to neighboring lands that have been used or developed. Great effort has been expended time and again to thwart development schemes incompatible with natural values. As voices for conservation and preservation grew, the competing land-use visions were often mutually exclusive. The map shows major development schemes —roads, reservoirs, railways, power plants, and ski resorts— that were promoted, debated, and defeated. Many progressed beyond planning and engineering stages even to beginning construction before they faltered or were stopped. Imagine a Cedar Grove Reservoir obliterating the floor and lower walls of Kings Canyon. A trans-Sierra highway over Kearsarge Pass would have cut in half the parks' backbone of high mountain wilderness. Miles on miles of Sierra Way road would intrude on scenic views from atop Moro Rock. A proposed highway from Lodgepole to Kings Canyon would have blocked eventual designation of national forest wilderness lands that now buffer the parks' wilderness areas along their western boundaries. The map on pages 108-109 shows the present network of roads and facilities in the two parks today.

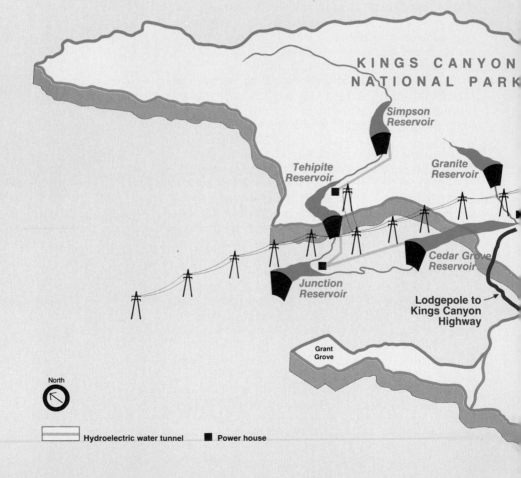

KINGS CANYON NATIONAL PARK

Simpson Reservoir

Tehipite Reservoir

Granite Reservoir

Cedar Grove Reservoir

Junction Reservoir

Lodgepole to Kings Canyon Highway

Grant Grove

North

▭ Hydroelectric water tunnel   ■ Power house

Mineral King Controversy

When the Forest Service granted Walt Disney's entertainment company a 30-year permit to develop a ski resort in the Mineral King Basin on national forest game refuge lands, the Sierra Club brought suit to block it. The suit did not succeed, but Congress added the lands to Sequoia National Park in 1978, ending the controversy. This painting shows the projected resort development in the basin.

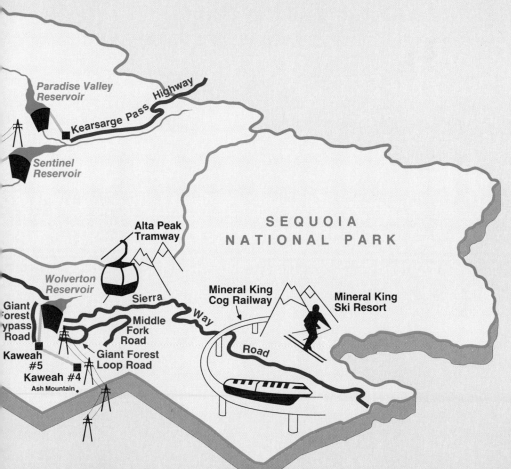

Paradise Valley Reservoir

Kearsarge Pass Highway

Sentinel Reservoir

Alta Peak Tramway

SEQUOIA NATIONAL PARK

Wolverton Reservoir

Sierra

Mineral King Cog Railway

Mineral King Ski Resort

Giant Forest Bypass Road

Way

Middle Fork Road

Kaweah #5

Giant Forest Loop Road

Road

Kaweah #4

Ash Mountain

Army Troops and the CCC

Sequoia National Park was created in 1890 with no provision to protect it. U.S. Army troops arrived in 1891 with little power except their presence. No enforcement powers existed to protect the fledgling national parks or forest reserves. With but a brief hiatus during the Spanish-American War, the Army ran Sequoia National Park through 1913. Their park accomplishments included building trails

and the 1903 completion of the road into Giant Forest. The troops' first problems came from poachers, cattlemen, and sheepherders. Despite lack of specific laws regarding national parks, Army personnel effectively controlled poaching and grazing trespass during their 23 years in the park. They would expel some grazing stock to rugged and far-distant park boundaries. When troops withdrew in October for the winter, the park had no

ready protection. Not until 1905 were employees in the parks and forest reserves empowered to make arrests. Walter Fry became acting civilian superintendent of Sequoia and General Grant national parks in 1912. He served as superintendent from 1914 to 1920. Congress authorized creation of the National Park Service in 1916 to manage and protect the growing number of parks.

CCC Built Park Facilities

Sequoia National Park benefitted greatly from the Civilian Conservation Corps (CCC) conceived by President Franklin D. Roosevelt in 1933 during the Great Depression. CCC crews built many roads and visitor facilities used today. They worked in parks and forests nationwide until 1942. At times more than 1,000 corpsman worked in the five CCC camps in Sequoia National Park. This corpsman creating a park sign earned $1 per day.

Tourism in the 19th Century

Recreation so dominates today's social values that we might assume it has enjoyed unbroken popularity from early civilizations forward. Not so. At the turn of this century, leisure time activities that did not "improve the day"—we would call them educational or cultural activities—were still suspect in Europe and North America. Old-time camping photographs that record the early recreational visitors to Sequoia National Park may startle us with the formality of the campers' dress. Men wore suit coats and white shirts with collars; women wore full dresses covering most of the neck as well as ankles. Their poses were necessarily stiff because slow contemporary photographic film required that subjects stand still and hold fixed expressions through long exposures. Slow and comparatively arduous travel by wagon did not inspire short stays by early tourists. Many campers stayed for several weeks and some for the entire summer season. Selecting a campsite could be more like staking a claim. In 1899 the acting military superintendent of Sequoia and General Grant national parks was Second Lt. Henry B. Clark. He reported rhetorically that year that Sequoia National Park was "a failure—a failure not because it wants in snow-clad peak, in noble game, in frightful precipice, deep gorge, or ragged canyon, but because the people find its beauties and its wonders inaccessible." In that year the park's only road was

a wagon road winding 11 miles toward Mineral King. Also in 1899 Tulare County businessmen and Visalia residents began to agitate for development of Sequoia National Park to boost the local economy. A newly formed Visalia Board of Trade toured Mineral King, Kern Canyon, Mount Whitney, and Giant Forest. With the group were a congressman and representatives of two railroads serving the region. The next year Congress appropriated $10,000 to

protect and improve Sequoia National Park. By late summer work was underway to extend an existing road to Giant Forest. The packers who outfitted the board of trade expedition had begun commercial packing the year before. They had set up tours to the Giant Forest with a tent hotel en route and a stage line operating between Visalia and their foothills ranch base. In 1899 these same packers opened Camp Sierra, a tent hotel in Giant Forest. By 1903 the Army had completed the

wagon road to Round Meadow and Moro Rock. The Big Trees were now comparatively accessible to tourists. While park facilities were still minimal, creation of the National Park Service, widespread automobile use, and the end of World War I soon would change that. Early visitors came by wagon or coach. The inset photos show early horseback travelers at a park entrance and a Sierra Club outing group.

Tourism in the Early 20th Century

With the road to Giant Forest completed in 1903, tourism soon began in earnest to Sequoia National Park as well as General Grant National Park. Trails were pushed out into Sequoia National Park, and Giant Forest was linked by trail with the Mineral King area. By 1907, the numbers of people summering at Giant Forest already justified opening a post office, and a telephone line was strung to Three Rivers. New problems with people began to occur, including ille-

gal hunting and camp sanitation. Many families stayed two months or more, escaping summer heat in the San Joaquin Valley. Their draft and saddle stock exacted a heavy toll on meadows near popular camping locations. Formal latrines soon had to be developed and grazing regulations instituted for stock. Backpacking still lay years in the future, but backcountry recreational use began to develop in the 1890s. Three Sierra Club members spearheaded backcountry recreation: Joseph N. LeConte, Bolton Coit Brown,

and Theodore Solomons. Solomons originated what became the John Muir Trail linking today's Sequoia and Kings Canyon National Parks with Yosemite National Park to the north. Sierra Club outings began in 1901 in Yosemite. In 1902 the club's second outing took some 200 members and 25,000 pounds of mule-transported dunnage to Kings Canyon. From their Copper Creek base camp, more than 50 clubbers ascended Mt. Brewer, which had severely tested

William Brewer and Clarence
King in the 1860s. Despite this
type of use, human impacts in
the backcountry would not become a critical issue until the
1960s. Not so with the parks'
developed areas. In 1913, the
Army's last year as caretaker
here, the first automobiles
entered Sequoia National
Park. A new era of tourism
was beginning. In that year
half of Sequoia National Park's
visitors came by wagon; six
percent came by car. In 1916
the National Park Service of
the U.S. Department of the

interior was established. By
1919 annual visits to both
Sequoia and General Grant
national parks had jumped
from an estimated 6,579 in
1913 to 52,017. Success
brought the need for protec-
tive controls on camping and
the development of water systems, garbage dumps, parking lots, amphitheaters, muse-
ums, and visitor centers. In
1920, Col. John R. White,
second civilian superintendent of the parks, reported that
"it was barely possible to see
Round Meadow because of
the tents which surrounded

it. Campers were using sequoia trees as braces for lean-
tos and tents. Construction of
organized government campgrounds got underway be-
tween 1921 and 1928. In 1970
the last campground in Giant
Forest closed, and Lodgepole
became Sequoia National
Park's primary camping area.
The large photo shows cars
parked near the museum in
Giant Forest about 1922. Insets
show a naturalist with visitors
on Moro Rock and two motor-
ists at Sentinel Tree in Giant
Forest Village about 1930.

Giant sequoia trees have evolved with wildfire, which plays a critical role in their successful reproduction.
Opposite: *Blackened accents of past fires persist beneath bark irregularities that prevent rainwater from washing them down. Fibrous, thick bark generally protects sequoia trees from significant damage in all but the hottest of wildfires.*

strategies. Competing fir and pine trees range generally from about 90 to 200 feet in height for mature trees. Giant sequoias average about 250 feet in height, and their lowest branches may occur 100 feet above the ground.

"This is speculation," Nichols says, "but sequoias may be favored by relatively hot fires. Tall giant sequoias whose foliage lies above the scorch zone tend to survive more than other, shorter species. Also, the hotter the fire, the better for the giant sequoia seedling that follows. Its chance of surviving is increased due to reduced shading in the post-fire environment." Many of the shorter, thin-barked trees that shade the forest floor are killed by fire. The heat also causes sequoia cones to dry out, open up, and then pop their seeds.

"For a giant sequoia tree," Nichols says, "successful reproduction just means you have to generate one replacement for yourself—and you have 2,000 years or more to do it."

Put that way, it would not seem difficult. Squirrels, beetles, and moths assure that a continuous supply of seed falls. However, without fire to open the forest floor and leave an ash seedbed, seedlings cannot develop. Nichols and other members of the parks' fire management team conduct prescribed burning. Their task is to mimic one of the effects of periodic natural fire, reducing accumulated fuel in the forest. Decades of fire suppression have allowed unnatural build-ups of woody material that could support unnatural fires that might damage the giant sequoias. As resource managers are able to return these areas to more natural fuel levels through the use of prescribed fire, they hope to allow natural fire to begin to resume more of its role in the creation and maintenance of sequoia habitat.

To understand this important aspect of managing national parks for natural values, you might consider taking a ranger-led walk in a prescribed burn area. Here among the hopeful show of new sequoia seedlings you can appreciate how today's park managers build on the traditions of George Stewart and John White in tending these sacred groves.

Wildflowers

Columbine

Jimson weed

Snow plant

Fiddleneck

Leopard lilies

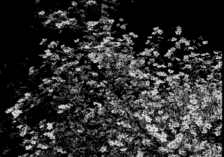

Pacific dogwood

Stonecrop

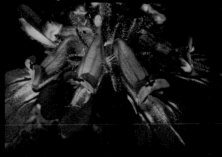

Sierra penstemon

Yellow-throated gilia

California poppies

White heather

Wild rose

Deadly nightshade

Monkeyflower

Wind poppy

Sierra gentian

The High Mountains:
Backcountry Choices

Traditionally, California marks the end of the westering urge—at least for the contiguous United States. Likewise, in our Nation's march west the Sierra Nevada looms as the penultimate mountain range. Westward across the San Joaquin Valley, only the Coast Range blocks the Pacific shore. For wilderness, however, the Sierra Nevada marks the last stopping point, and doubly so for wilderness mountain climbers.

Norman Clyde was attracted to these mountains sometime after 1911 while in his mid-20s. The High Sierra was to become for him, as Walt Wheelock writes, "as familiar as one's own back yard." Clyde spent more than 50 years perfecting his mental maps, locating crashed airplanes, and rescuing lost souls and climbers in trouble—or retrieving their bodies.

Clyde's name was legendary. Many climbers would rank him second only to John Muir as an intimate pioneer of places inaccessible and second to none as a climber. Apart from legend few people knew much about this quiet man who minimized his achievements. Asked about his climbing feats, Clyde might downplay them by saying they weren't really so many when you considered that he was 350 years old.

Recollecting Clyde's feats, Wheelock wrote in 1961: "A strong team of skilled rockclimbers will conquer a lonely spire, using the most modern of climbing gear and techniques and win through with well co-ordinated teamwork to find on a faded Kodak box the record of a solo climb of three decades ago. Or, at the high point of a distant ridge will be found a small cairn, but no written record. Obviously the work of man, and one mountaineer will turn to his companion with, 'Well, it looks like a first ascent, except for Norman Clyde.' Later, discussing the route with him, Clyde will ponder a bit, ask a couple of questions about some difficult pitch encountered on the ascent, then admit he had been there a score of years ago."

Norman Clyde climbed Mt. Whitney at least 50 times. Between 1914 and about 1940, he became the first climber to reach the tops of at least 126 peaks. Clyde Minaret (first ascent June 1928) near today's Devils Postpile National Monument and Clyde Spires (first ascents north and south peaks July 1933) on the northeast boundary of Kings Canyon National Park are named for him. Other than his carefully crafted newspaper and magazine accounts of climbs and the few recorded recollections of fellow mountaineers, Norman Clyde's long High Sierra tenure passed with sparse biographic record. Not so Clyde's backpacks. Heading for the mountain backcountry one day Clyde, weighing 140 pounds then, weighed his pack: 75 pounds. He spent that night with a survey crew amazed at the size of his pack. In the morning, the crewmen badgered Clyde about the dangers of running out of food in the wilderness. First one survey crewman and then another urged "extra" cans of their food on Clyde. By the time Clyde set out again his pack had grown to 95 pounds!

"I can still remember my awe at the collection of gear Norman drew out of his duffle bag," recollects climbing companion Smoke Blanchard. "There's part of the weight right there. The duffle bag was lashed to a six-pound Yukon pack frame which also supported a full length Hudson Bay axe. But perhaps the kitchen bag was the most surprising . . . Norman's six large kettles, the cups and spoons, the dishes and bowls, the salt shakers, condiments, servers, and graters, and, for all I know, cookie cutters. . . . Boots? He carried several; ski boots, tricouni boots, rubber-soled boots for the rocks, camp slippers."

"It's not true," Clyde told Blanchard once, "that I carry an anvil in my pack." He did carry *five* cameras: two 35mms, two 120s, and a spare. *And the books!* Smoke Blanchard recalls "Norman's rather large library in many languages"—in his pack, not in his cabin. Clyde read Spanish, French, German, Italian, Latin, and Greek. On long trips he treasured the Greek. He was most rusty in it; books in Greek lasted longer.

"I think many people might find his way of travel in the mountains quite strange, especially with today's gear," Blanchard comments, "but you see, Norman was not just visiting the mountains or passing through the peaks. He lived there. . . ."

Backpacking boomed in the parks' backcountry in the 1970s, as an aged Clyde took his last Sierra trips. The statistics are staggering. Under the heading "The Baby Boomers and the Backcountry," historians Dilsaver and Tweed lay them out in their definitive resource history, *Challenge of the Big Trees*:

"The combination of unprecedented numbers of young people, increasing environmental awareness, and great strides in the quality of backpacking equipment resulted in the single most drastic short-term use increase borne by the two parks during their first century. In 1962, 8,054 people entered the backcountry of the two parks; thirteen years later, the comparable figure totaled 48,207, an increase of nearly 600 percent."

By comparison to Clyde's packing habits, post-Earth Day backpackers had a feather-light fetish. Pride just short of chauvinism saw them shave further mere *ounces* from their gear between trips. Many would set off with a tent, pack, and sleeping bag whose combined weight would hardly tip the scales against Clyde's bare Yukon packframe.

Ironically, the new backpackers, among their other environmental impacts, further *extended* the range of the parks' black bears. This posed one more thorny issue for park managers wrestling with maximizing natural systems. What is natural? Or *when* was it natural? Or when did it *become* natural? The more we learn, the more perplexing some such questions become. For example, black bears expanded their range following the killing of the last California grizzly bears by 1922. "The foothills chaparral was grizzly habitat, not black bear habitat," says bear specialist Dave Graber, a scientist with the National Park Service's Southern Sierra Research Center in Sequoia National Park. "Black bears were confined to the mid-elevation forests. The foothills belonged to the grizzly. Alpine habitats were almost vacant."

Once the grizzly bears were extinct locally, black bears expanded their range downward, taking advantage of their vacated niche. In the 1970s the backpacker legions advanced into the high Sierra, and black bears soon followed the food higher into the mountains.

"This is an artificially created niche in alpine habitat," Graber explains. "Protein is the limiting factor for the bears' range. The alpine backcountry

Sierra mountaineer Norman Clyde displays his ice ax and tricouni boots at a rest stop on one of his countless climbs in the first half of this century. "The old gaffer," as he styled himself, scaled Mt. Whitney more than 50 times and logged at least 126 first ascents. Several peaks and spires from near Devils Postpile National Monument southward into these parks are named for Norman Clyde.

Crystal Cave

Crystal Cave is among the most beautiful of the nearly 100 marble solution caves in the parks. Among readily accessible caves in this region, it offers relatively undisturbed formations. Other larger caves in southern California, Lilburn and Church caves, are not readily accessible. Crystal Cave's estimated 10,000 feet of passageways occur in a formation of limestone that has metamorphosed under tremendous heat and pressure into marble. This formation measures only 800 to 900 feet long, 300 feet wide, and 200 feet tall. Seepage of slightly acidic groundwater through the formation has dissolved the marble to create the passageways and cave rooms. With four entrances and so much passageway, Crystal Cave is maze-like in character. Marble Hall measures 175 feet long, 60 feet wide, and is 30 to 40 feet high in the area that visitors tour. Regular cave tours are operated in summer for a fee by the nonprofit Sequoia Natural History Association. Tours last 50 minutes and cover ½ mile via a loop trail, including the popular Organ Room and Dome Room formations. Tour leaders explain the geology and biology of the cave. It is a steep half-mile walk one way from the parking lot to the cave entrance. The trail is not recommended for persons in poor physical condition.

An Underground World

Two fishermen, Park Service employees A. L. Medley and C. N. Webster, discovered Crystal Cave in 1918. The cave is located below Giant Forest in Sequoia National Park. Inside the cave the temperature is 48°F. Rooms and passageways offer the bizarre shapes of stalactites, stalagmites, draperies, flowstone, and other cave decorations. More than 100 known caves honeycomb these parks.

High Mountain Meadows

Southern California's most direct link with the Arctic lies among its southern Sierra peaks in their beautiful high meadows. This alpine vegetation shares so many features with the tundra in the Far North that it has been called alpine tundra. Scientists in these parks classify these meadows as either montane or alpine. If the meadows are in the mixed conifer forest, they are montane. If the meadows are above treeline they are alpine. Montane meadows are lower in elevation and more productive than the alpine meadows. As Ice Age glaciers retreated northward and climate warmed, islands of tundra were left high on mountain flanks. Only on high mountains do local climates now resemble that of the Arctic. However, only 10 percent of Sierran alpine flora is the same as that throughout circumpolar regions. Severe climates and short-lived growing seasons make alpine meadows fragile landscapes. Highly susceptible to damage by horses, mules, and hikers today, they were damaged severely in the last century by domestic sheep grazing throughout the Sierra. John Muir decried the destruction wreaked by domestic sheep—he called them "hoofed locusts." So extensive was the damage that researchers debate whether truly natural meadows still exist. "Some meadows have not been grazed for several decades, but we must assume that the sheep were everywhere and left no meadows untouched," says a park scientist. "We really don't know what an untouched meadow looked like. The best thing we can do is to let things occur unimpeded for a time and see what results." Unfortunately, the earliest photographs of these meadows were taken after domestic sheep grazing began. The large photo shows a meadow in the Dusy Basin in Kings Canyon National Park. The inset photo shows California Conservation Corps workers rehabilitating a damaged meadow.

Mountain life above treeline shares many characteristics with life in deserts. Here plants and animals must adapt to severe conditions of wind, cold, and shortages of moisture. Above 14,000 feet in the Sierra few plants grow taller than lichens on bare rock. Most plants adapt to high elevations through dwarfism and strategies to avoid dehydration, such as growing in low-lying matted configurations and having waxy or hair-covered leaves and stems that retard moisture loss. Near-constant winds and very low humidity on high mountains would rapidly suck moisture out of unprotected plants. Some plants must also preserve warmth during the brief growing season. Growing low to the ground helps tremendously because air temperatures drop significantly just inches above the ground. At 11,000 feet on a sunny day the air 5 feet above the ground may be 20 degrees Fahrenheit cooler than the air at ground level. You can test this yourself in the highcountry: compare both wind and air temperature sensations as you first stand on a rock facing into the wind and then lie down on that rock. Sun rays can damage plant tissue, too. Some plants of the high mountains have evolved reddish-brown colorations to block the solar radiation that Earth's atmosphere screens out only partially at high elevations. Animals generally respond to mountain rigors by behavioral adaptations rather than by changes in their bodies. Because they can fly, birds pick and choose elevations daily for feeding, nesting, drinking, and other activities. Two small mountain mammals cope

Plants and animals of the mountain world:
1 Golden eagle
2 Pika
3 Yellow-bellied marmot
4 Bighorn sheep, ram

5 Alpine buckwheat
6 Whitebark pine
7 Whitebark pine, krummholz
8 White heather
9 Dwarf willow

with long winters by varied strategies. Yellow-bellied marmots store body fat—they can double their weight in a summer — and hibernate, slowly burning the body fat over winter. Pikas store plant matter in miniature haystacks they eat throughout winter. Both must be on guard against golden eagles that, given the opportunity, prey on them. Since park roads do not go above 7,800 feet, most visitors do not experience the parks' alpine realms. Above 9,000 feet the climate is too harsh to support either tall trees or dense forests. Generally, above 11,000 feet no trees can grow. However, winter snow cover helps protect low-growing plants like a shield. Alpine animals breathe air with less than half the oxygen content of air at sea level.

10 Map lichen
11 Rosy Finch
12 Sierra primrose
13 Campion or catchfly
14 Spreading phlox

just didn't have it—until the backpackers' food supplies showed up."

Suddenly it was worth the bears' energy investment to range the highcountry. Protein is protein, freeze-dried or not. Bears are opportunistic feeders: they scavenge a camp, garner its garbage, or bamboozle a backpacker into throwing a pack at them. Problems between bears and people increased, although Graber says such incidents apparently have stabilized since backpacking numbers peaked at more than 48,000 in 1975. (In 1990, 32,000 persons used the parks' backcountry.) Also, park managers have moved decisively to separate bears from human food supplies, which too often spell trouble, ultimately for the bears.

This was not the first time protein has been artificially added to the mountain realms. The lack of fish in highcountry lakes rankled many early anglers. Most of these gem-like lakes had been fish-free since the retreat of Ice Age glaciers. Many lakes that might support trout featured outlets too steep for fish to conquer from lower, unglaciated waters. Fish planting began in the 1850s and by the 1870s was widespread. Anglers might catch a few trout, put them in a bucket, and release them in the next higher lake. Over the years fish planting became the policy of most land managers, including those in the National Park Service. Today the policy has been reversed in Sequoia and Kings Canyon National Parks in a first step toward restoring their aquatic ecosystems to more natural conditions. Along with fish, many bait organisms and exotic plants were also introduced into lakes and further upset the natural communities.

Paul Fodor may have made more multiple visits to a variety of mountain lakes than any person since Norman Clyde. Until 1991 the Sierra District (read "backcountry") ranger with 16 years of experience in these parks, Fodor studied wildlife management at what is now California State University, Long Beach. He began his Park Service career at Death Valley and transferred here in 1974.

On a recent flyover of the two parks, Fodor's last name—the same as the world-renowned travel guidebook series—was not lost on his photographer co-passenger. For two hours they flew above the parks from below Sequoia National Park's south boundary to Golden Trout Lake above Kings Canyon National Park's north boundary. Fodor consulted the map only twice while calling out place names—peaks, passes, lakes, streams, canyons, and geological features—for the mountainscapes endlessly unfolding below. And he did so even though he had spent half of the night in a hospital emergency room, having lost the tip of a finger in an accident. Virtually everything Fodor mentioned from this map-like airborne perspective he had personally ground-truthed at one time or another.

Park boundaries, except perhaps for those following the Sierra Crest, are essentially invisible even from the air. Increasingly, they also become less and less dividing lines where they delineate changes in federal agencies' jurisdictions. Wilderness designations that overlap agency boundaries have helped "break down" these dividing lines. The 1964 federal Wilderness Act and subsequent federal legislation known as the California Wilderness Act of 1984 have also given increased impetus to natural management within the parks. The 1984 law designated some 85 percent of the parks as wilderness, "where the earth and its community of life are untrammeled by man, where man himself is a visitor who does not remain." The 1964 Wilderness Act mandated that such land be "protected and managed so as to preserve its natural conditions. . . ."

Wilderness legislation set a broader social context for the science-driven impulse to manage parklands for natural values and to restore natural ecosystems. Today the parks and their designated wilderness areas in places join wilderness areas on the Inyo, Sierra, and Sequoia national forests. These situations have inspired cooperation between federal land managers and have helped foster interagency wilderness management initiatives throughout the central Sierra Nevada.

National park management emphasizes the values of preservation and enjoyment. National forest managers pursue multiple use, a land-use concept encompassing logging, mining, hunting, grazing, and recreational development. However, the more restrictive wilderness designation makes some park and forest lands subject to similar management practices. Still, variations in park and forest regulations can confuse backpackers ignorant of the bound-

Stephen T. Mather, left, stands atop Mt. Whitney with Emerson Hough, who later wrote the buckskin classic, The Covered Wagon. *Hough helped publicize the growing national parks movement that Mather promoted tirelessly. This photograph was taken by Gilbert H. Grosvenor, editor of* National Geographic Magazine, *on a 1915 trip that Mather organized to promote creation of the National Park Service. The National Geographic Society soon contributed funds that enabled the Federal Government to buy important parcels of private land in the Giant Forest. And, in 1916, Mather became the first director of the new National Park Service.*

Air pollution proves the error of thinking of national parks as islands of protected natural land. Three major air quality problems—visibility impairment, acid deposition, and harmful ozone concentration—link the parks to larger ecosystems. Possible global warming also could alter park environments radically. Air in the San Joaquin Valley generally exceeds federal and state health and welfare standards for carbon monoxide, ozone, and particulates. Summertime airflows in the valley transport pollutants from north to south through heavily urbanized and agricultural areas to the parks. At night, eddying air currents recirculate pollutants below about 1,000 feet in elevation. In the afternoon, upslope, up-valley winds carry the pollutants into the parks. These pollutants may stay in the valley anywhere from three days to several weeks. The Eleven Range Overlook, Moro Rock, and other vantage points readily show how air pollution blocks scenic views. Air pollution acidifies rain and snow falling on the parks. Air pollu-tants that cause acid deposition come from the burning of fossil fuels. Sierran lakes are more sensitive to acids than lakes in the northeastern United States. Spring snow-melt and late summer storm pH levels in the parks can harm aquatic organisms.

San Francisco

C A L I F

Ozone Injury to Trees

Of all western national parks, Sequoia and Kings Canyon contain the highest levels of visible ozone injury to Jeffrey and ponderosa pines. To investigate ozone injury to giant sequoias, researchers enclosed and fumigated tree branches with three concentrations of ozone. Level one is ambient ozone—the amount now in the air. Level two (2x) subjects trees to two times that concentration and level three to (3x). These studies will show how ozone affects the trees' physiology *both at today's concentrations and if ozone pollution worsens. In studies of giant sequoia seedlings, 1.5x concentrations reduced photosynthesis rates by 44 percent. If ozone pollution increases even a little bit, the seedling growth rates will decline markedly. Ozone injury on giant sequoia seedlings and on yellow pines shows as yellow-green banding on needles. These parks experience some of California's highest ozone concentrations.*

Pollution Blocks the View

Good views of the Silliman Crest and Moro Rock from Milk Ranch Fire Lookout occur a few days a year (left photo). Air pollution is to blame. Pollutants scatter light rays to create a haze, reducing visibility (right photo). Because of air circulation patterns, the pollution at points in the parks may be more severe than in areas where pollutants originate.

Just How Dry Is It?

Research in Sequoia National Park is rewriting California's climate history. Studies of tree-ring growth indicate that what we thought was a drought may be the normal condition. A new 1,000-year record of Sierra Nevada temperature and precipitation suggests that 20th-century weather has been unusually wet and warm.

The record shows 1932 to 1981 as one of the wettest periods in the past thousand years. The cycle of dry winters that began in 1986 may be a return to more typical conditions. Californians may have to adjust their lifestyles for a drier future.

SIERRA

OWENS VALLEY

Fresno

NEVADA

Mount Whitney

JOAQUIN

Visalia

GREAT WESTERN DIVIDE

VALLEY

Tulare Lake bed

RNIA

AN

RANGES

Buena Vista Lake bed

TEHACHAPI MOUNTAINS

Los Angeles

Diane Ewell manages the parks' air quality program. "Because of the nature of air pollution, improvements will only be possible through everyone's involvement," she says. "We emphasize public education. Most people do not understand how much the parks are at risk." Ewell holds a master's degree in ecology from the University of California, Davis, specializing in air pollution transport. She previously worked as a fire monitor here and on fire studies in Yosemite National Park.

David Graber is recognized as the foremost expert on Sierran black bears. He leads the parks' efforts to inventory natural resources for developing a computerized information system—see the following pages. This map-like database enables the parks' managers to make scientifically informed decisions. Graber also contributes to acid deposition research. He holds a Ph.D. in wildland resource science from the University of California, Berkeley.

Diane Ewell studies air pollution problems. The photo below shows a technician with fumigation chambers used in researching effects of ozone pollution on sequoias.

David Graber's inventories of natural resources provide information to measure and predict future impacts of events and actions on park ecosystems.

David Parsons orchestrates research regarding how global climate change will affect national parks in the Sierra Nevada. He specializes in the dynamic relationships between climate, fire, and living things. He has coordinated acid deposition research and studied forest and chaparral fire ecology. His studies of wilderness impacts led to the parks' trailhead quota system. Parsons holds a Ph.D. in population biology-plant ecology from Stanford University.

Thomas Swetnam uses tree-ring analysis to reconstruct long-term histories of forest fires and insect outbreaks. Patterns help identify links between these events and climate changes. Swetnam is developing millennia-long fire histories of giant sequoia groves throughout the Sierra Nevada. Swetnam holds a Ph.D. in forestry-watershed management from the University of Arizona, where he serves as assistant professor in the Laboratory of Tree-Ring Research.

David Parsons has pursued park science since 1973. In the photo a technician collects data on lake water chemistry for acid precipitation studies that Parsons managed.

Officially known as dendrochronology, Thomas Swetnam's tree-ring analysis reconstructs more than 2,000 years of fire history in giant sequoia groves.

Geographic Information System

Satellites and sometimes footsore, backpacking National Park Service scientists may seem unlikely partners in the application of science to park management in a world of high technology. However, using Geographic Information Systems (GIS), the scientists can create computerized theme maps drawn from diverse data sources. Sources include satellite remote sensing imagery, field research, and inventories from historical records in park files, books, and technical journals. GIS provides sophisticated tools for savvy park management. Imagine, for example, that you want to pick the best location in the park for a new campground. GIS can combine map-based information on the themes of (1) topography, (2) vegetation, (3) soils, (4) geology, (5) streams, (6) roads, and (7) wildlife sightings. From these sets of themes a new map can be drawn that addresses their combined concerns. Park managers can use the new map to identify likely level and appropriately wooded spots that offer good drainage, a stream nearby, and road access—and that contain no endangered plant species and lie at least one mile from the nearest nesting sites of endangered birds. Using GIS-generated maps, fire managers can predict the probable behavior of a fire in a ponderosa pine forest on a mountain slope at a given elevation under certain weather and wind conditions. Search and rescue teams might develop a map-based model for finding lost hikers. GIS is a promising new tool for managing national parks.

A New Management Tool

A research biologist and the parks' superintendent use the Geographic Information System database to explore potential impacts of alternative management strategies on a variety of natural resources. GIS enables quantities of formerly isolated information to be integrated for the purpose of answering specific questions that managers confront in day-to-day operations of the parks and in planning for their future.

With winter's onset, snow softens higher-elevation landscapes, blending forest types and lending them a visual evenness of beauty. Californians closely follow reports of Sierran snowpack: both residential and agricultural water supplies for the coming year depend on it.

aries and their management implications. Agencies now cooperate to achieve as much consistency in rules and management practices as possible.

Philosophically, recreation has taken second place to natural values in parklands management. Realistically, however, the economics of parklands remain heavily weighted toward visitor services and facilities. In the backcountry, people management can be a prerequisite to managing natural resources; witness the successful backcountry use permit system begun here in 1972. This is especially true in mountainous wilds where every elevation gain finds more fragile, more vulnerable habitats. The veneer of life thins to a mere membrane across this mountain domain where even the air can be rarefied.

Norman Clyde, with his backpack library and aversion to bureaucracy, could have invented the word *rarefied*. It can mean both "rare and thin" or "made more spiritual, refined." It can also mean "very light." As Michael Cohen writes in *The Pathless Way*, his account of John Muir's spiritual journey, "Going light requires that a man cease to use any method of perception which mediates between himself and Nature." Norman Clyde was one of Cohen's first mountain teachers. He must have imparted high standards. Such direct vision of nature as Cohen demands strikes most of us as unattainable, seeming as unlikely as being mistaken for a boulder by a golden eagle as it prepares to land.

This in fact happened to Norman Clyde—and not once but twice.

Part 3

Guide and Adviser

By Car Sequoia and Kings Canyon National Parks protect the southern Sierra Nevada where this great range culminates in Mount Whitney, elevation 14,494 feet. No roads cross these parks; they can be reached by automobile only from the west, and accessibility varies with the season. Highway 198 leads into Sequoia National Park from Visalia, Calif. Highway 180 leads into Kings Canyon National Park from Fresno. If you don't care for steep, winding roads or are driving a large vehicle, you may prefer Highway 180 instead of 198. The Generals Highway connects these routes in the parks, making a loop trip possible. Highway 180 is known as the Kings Canyon Highway. It comes to a dead end—hardly an appropriate term in such a glorious setting!—in its namesake beyond Cedar Grove.

At the entrance stations you will be asked to pay a fee. You may choose to purchase a Golden Eagle Pass there. Good for a calendar year, the pass covers entrance fees at all federal fee areas in the United States.

Once in the parks, private vehicles are necessary for motorized travel except for guided tours of Kings Canyon and Giant Forest; see **Sequoia Guest Services** on page 110. Vehicle rentals are available in Fresno and Visalia.

Winter Road Closures Highway 180 into Cedar Grove is closed at the Hume Lake junction from early November to late April. The Mineral King Road from Highway 198 into southern Sequoia National Park is closed two miles below Atwell Mill with the first heavy snow or around Thanksgiving. The Buckeye Flat/Middle Fork Trailhead Road is closed from mid-October until mid-April when the Buckeye Flat campground closes. The lower Crystal Cave Road is closed when the cave is closed

in September. Its upper two miles, as well as the Panoramic Point and Moro Rock-Crescent Meadow roads, are closed with the first heavy snow. Spring opening dates depend on the weather.

Road and weather information is available 24 hours a day by calling 209-565-3351. The recording is updated about 9 a.m. daily.

Gasoline and Service Stations Gasoline is available at Lodgepole, Grant Grove, and Cedar Grove. Minor auto-repair services are provided year round at Lodgepole and Grant Grove. Diesel fuel is available at Lodgepole. Propane is available at Lodgepole and Grant Grove.

Driving Times Plan on approximate driving times as follows. **From Ash Mountain**: to Crystal Cave, 1¼ hours; to Lodgepole, 1 hour; to Visalia, 1 hour. **From Lodgepole to Grant Grove**: 1 hour. **From Grant Grove**: to Cedar Grove, 1 hour; to Fresno, 1¼ hours. **From Highway 198 to Mineral King**: at least 1 hour. **Rough Roads** are:

Photo pages 104-105: *Below Tokopah Falls*

Crystal Cave Road, no buses, motor homes, or trailers; Mineral King Road, no trailers; Redwood Saddle Road, trailers, buses, and motor homes not recommended. **Narrow Roads** are: Crystal Cave, Mineral King, Panoramic Point, Redwood Saddle, and Crescent Meadow roads. **Length Advisory:** Vehicles over 22 feet long not advised between Highway 198 and Giant Forest. See **Safe Driving** on page 123.

Where's the Drive-through Tree? Not here. The giant sequoia that you could drive through, the Wawona Tree, *was* in Yosemite National Park, but it fell down in 1969.

By Air Fresno Airport and car rentals there offer the closest major connection to the park via either Highway 180 or 198. Allow 2 hours driving time from Fresno to the Ash Mountain entrance of Sequoia National Park via Highways 99 and 198 through Visalia. Allow 1¼ hours driving time from Fresno to the Big Stump entrance of Kings Canyon National Park at Grant Grove. Some flights land at Visalia Airport, one hour from Ash Mountain via Highway 198. Car rentals are available at the airport.

By Bus or Rail No public transportation serves the parks. Buses and AMTRAK serve Fresno and Visalia. Small tour companies outside the parks can provide access. For current information about such services call the parks (telephone numbers on page 110).

Motorcycles Motorcyclists should avoid the oil buildup in the center of the uphill lane on park roads.

Bicycles Highways in the parks are hilly and winding with road shoulders not suited for bicycle traffic. Bicycles must follow the same rules of the road as cars. Bicycles are not permitted on any trails or cross-country. Ask for printed bicycling information and restrictions at visitor centers or by mail.

Sierran Weather The foothills are characterized by mild, wet winters and hot, dry summers. August lows average 67°F there; August highs average 96 and often exceed 100. January lows average 36; the average high is 57. In the middle elevations, where the sequoias grow, August lows average 50, highs 76. January nighttime temperatures average 24 and daytime highs 42. Snow may linger into June at this elevation. Above 9,000 feet in elevation August nighttime temperatures average in the mid-30s and may drop below freezing any month. Winter temperatures at higher elevations average in the mid-30s during the day and below 10 at night.

Daytime thundershowers can occur. **Always** be prepared for sudden wet, cold weather and resultant hazards of hypothermia, the rapid and often fatal lowering of body temperature.

Sequoia and Kings Canyon National Parks

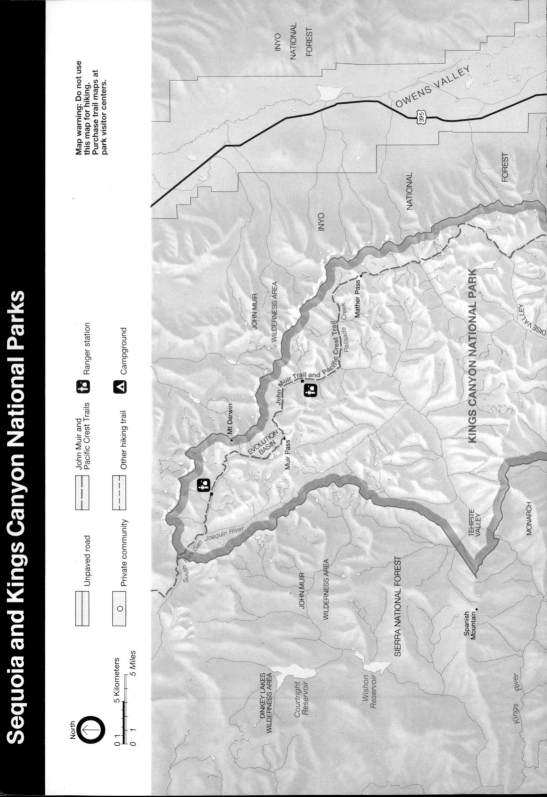

North

0 1 5 Kilometers
0 1 5 Miles

Unpaved road

John Muir and
Pacific Crest Trails

Other hiking trail

Private community

Ranger station

Campground

Map warning: Do not use
this map for hiking.
Purchase trail maps at
park visitor centers.

INYO NATIONAL FOREST

OWENS VALLEY

395

INYO NATIONAL FOREST

JOHN MUIR WILDERNESS AREA

Mt Darwin

EVOLUTION BASIN

Muir Pass

John Muir Trail and Pacific Crest Trail

Palisade Creek

Mather Pass

KINGS CANYON NATIONAL PARK

South Fork San Joaquin River

JOHN MUIR WILDERNESS AREA

SIERRA NATIONAL FOREST

TEHIPITE VALLEY

MONARCH

PARADISE VALLEY

Spanish Mountain

DINKEY LAKES WILDERNESS AREA

Courtright Reservoir

Wishon Reservoir

Kings River

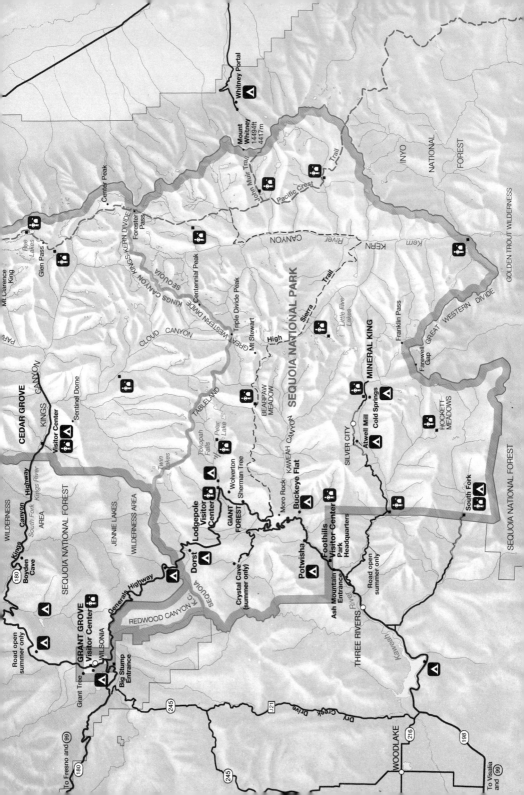

Addresses and Telephone Numbers
All telephone numbers are area code 209 unless listed otherwise.

National Park Service Sequoia and Kings Canyon National Parks, Three Rivers, CA 93271. For visitor information call 565-3134. For information on backcountry permits call 565-3708. For recorded information on road and weather conditions call 565-3351. For Grant Grove information call 335-2856. The parks' 24-hour dispatch and business phone number is 565-3341. **In case of emergency dial 911** from any phone in the park. No coins required.

Sequoia Natural History Association, Ash Mountain Box 10, Three Rivers CA 93271, 565-3758. Call this number for information about books, trail maps, and other items available for sale. Purchases support this nonprofit membership organization that contributes extensively to the parks' educational and scientific programs. The association also sponsors field seminars and other special activities that supplement National Park Service interpretive programs. Catalogs and brochures for the association's publications and programs and membership information are available at visitor centers or by mail.

The Sequoia and Kings Canyon National Parks Foundation, Ash Mountain Box 10, Three Rivers, CA 93271, 565-3758. The foundation conducts campaigns to fund special projects within the parks. It funded completion of the Trail for All People and is working to fund rehabilitation of the General Sherman Tree area. Ask for information about the foundation at a visitor center or write.

Camping reservations can be made by phone for one campground for part of the year. See pages 114-115.

Sequoia Guest Services, P.O. Box 789, Three Rivers, CA 93271, 561-3314. Call this number for information and reservations for lodgings in the parks. Lodgings are available at Giant Forest and Grant Grove and in summer only at Cedar Grove and Stony Creek. (Stony Creek is operated by the same concessioner in Sequoia National Forest between Giant Forest and Grant Grove.) Advance reservations are advisable. In summer motor tours of Giant Forest and Kings Canyon are offered, and Bearpaw High Sierra Camp rents its tent-top cabins. In winter this concessioner offers ski touring and rentals in Giant Forest and Grant Grove. For information about these concessions call 565-3381.

Park Newspaper Current activities, events, facilities, services, and safety information are listed in the parks' free *Sequoia Bark* newspaper. Pick up a copy at any entrance or ranger station, visitor center, or concession accommodation. Each issue also offers feature articles of seasonal interest to park travelers. The newspaper is published several times each year to keep information current.

Services for Visitors with Disabilities
Information on accessibility is provided on request by mail or at visitor centers. Several campsites in the parks have been altered to increase their accessibility.

Religious Services In summer religious services are presented in various parts of the parks. Check the *Sequoia Bark* for schedules.

Stop at a visitor center as you enter the parks. At Ash Mountain the visitor center is on the right one mile uphill from the entrance station on Highway 198. Grant Grove Visitor Center is two miles from the Big Stump Entrance on Highway 180; past the entrance station bear left, following the signs. Midway between these two is Lodgepole Visitor Center, near Giant Forest in Sequoia National Park. Visitor centers are open from 8 or 9 a.m. to 4:30 or 5 p.m. They offer information on campsite availability, road and trail conditions, and weather. Their audiovisual programs and exhibits describe features and things you can see and do in keeping with your itinerary. Rangers at the information desks can answer your questions and advise you on the most profitable use of your time in the parks. A ranger can also help you match activities to your fitness level. Books and maps sold at visitor centers are both effective planning tools and good souvenirs for extending the enjoyment of your trip after you leave the parks. Publications are sold by the nonprofit Sequoia Natural History Association as a service to visitors and to benefit National Park Service programs.

Foothills Visitor Center Just inside the southern entrance of the parks, Foothills Visitor Center provides information services, exhibits, sales of maps and other publications, first aid, and local backcountry permits. Schedules of ranger-led walks and programs are available, as are Golden Access and Golden Age Passports. These passes are for U.S. citizens who have disabilities or are 62 years and over. In cooperation with the Sequoia Natural History Association, the parks are planning to renovate and enlarge this visitor center. New exhibits will focus on resource

issues facing these parks as they move into their second century of existence. At approximately 1,700 feet in elevation, the visitor center sits in the Mediterranean climate of the west slope Sierran foothills.

Lodgepole Visitor Center Located just beyond Giant Forest on the beautiful Marble Fork of the Kaweah River, Lodgepole Visitor Center provides a full range of information services. Exhibits and audiovisual programs present the early history of the park from settlers and explorers to loggers and the U.S. Army. Hale Tharp settled Giant Forest, which was named by early park advocate John Muir. Army Capt. Charles Young, a black graduate of West Point, spent only one year, 1903, in Sequoia National Park but oversaw important work on its road system. Geology exhibits explain the global phenomenon of plate tectonics and its relationship to the uplift of the Sierra Nevada, which was shaped by various forms of erosion, including glaciation.

Grant Grove Visitor Center Located in the portion of Kings Canyon National Park that was once the small General Grant National Park, Grant Grove Visitor Center provides full information services and audiovisual programs. Its exhibits feature the National Park Service in California, map sections of the parks, local logging history, giant sequoia ecology, park founders, and the national park idea. Its Sequoia Room gives you an in-the-round idea of the size of a giant sequoia. There are also exhibits on the General Grant Tree and Grant Grove.

Cedar Grove Ranger Station Open in summer only, the historic log ranger station at Cedar Grove provides information services, sales of maps and other publications, first aid, and backcountry permits. (In summer, from 7 a.m. to 3 p.m., backcountry permits are issued at the kiosk at Roads End.) If you travel to Cedar Grove, stop at Grant Grove Visitor Center first to take advantage of its audiovisual programs and exhibits.

Mineral King Ranger Station From about June to mid-September, the ranger station at Mineral King also provides information services, sales of maps and other publications, first aid, and backcountry permits. A montane valley reached by one steep, narrow road, Mineral King provides popular trailheads for mountain backcountry destinations. Mineral King Road is **not** a recommended drive for casual sightseeing, RVs, or trailers.

Interpretive, Educational Activities Ranger-led walks and evening programs are offered daily in summer and on weekends and holidays the rest of the year. Activity schedules are posted at visitor centers, ranger stations, and bulletin boards and are published in summer issues of the *Sequoia Bark*. Meeting places for programs and walks may be at campgrounds or other locations.

In Sequoia National Park, programs are offered in the foothills, Mineral King, and the Giant Forest, Lodgepole, and Dorst areas.

In Kings Canyon the programs are held in the Grant Grove and Cedar Grove areas.

Interpretive activities can be a memorable park experience. Some may open your eyes to park management issues, or delight you with insights into the lives of park wildlife. Topics may include bears, birdlife, the Big Trees, geology, fire ecology, air quality, park history, John Muir, foothills chaparral, rivers, Sierran meadows, Indians, and demonstrations of firefighting, backpacking, and horsepacking. Check for special children's programs. Some programs are accessible to those in wheelchairs; these are identified in the *Sequoia Bark*.

Field Seminars Each year the nonprofit Sequoia Natural History Association sponsors field seminars in the parks. Experts in birdlife, wildflowers, backpacking, and the parks' history lead two- and three-day or longer outdoor encounters with a variety of natural and cultural features. Some seminars involve backpacking or camping. For others, lodgings can be taken with the parks' concessioner. Field seminars are offered in spring and summer and again in winter. For information or registration write or call the Sequoia Natural History Association as listed on page 110.

Nature Center Open daily in July and August, the Nature Center at Lodgepole affords children of all ages a hands-on natural experience. Additional activities and programs for children, including nature walks and campfire programs, either start or take place here.

Backpacking by the Rae Lakes

A hiker at Franklin Pass

Crosscountry skiing

Pack train on Glen Pass

Historic Muir Hut on Muir Pass

At the General Sherman Tree

Overnight accommodations in the parks range from public campgrounds and the Bearpaw Meadow Backcountry Camp, through rustic sleeping cabins without baths and deluxe cabins with fireplaces, to motel units. Information and reservations for all overnight accommodations except campgrounds can be obtained from **Guest Services**—see page 110. **Advance reservations are advisable**, especially in summer or on holiday weekends.

Food services range from sandwich and soup outlets through cafeterias and restaurants. Major visitor services areas in the parks offer limited retail food markets. **Giant Forest Village** Cafeteria, Lodge Dining Room (summer only), and Fireside Room (sandwiches only, *after cafeteria and dining room are closed*). **Wolverton** Soup and sandwich service *in ski season only*. **Lodgepole** Deli and Ice Cream Shop (summer only). Lodgepole is a major campground area, and food-to-go is a specialty in the Deli. **Stony Creek** Restaurant (summer only). **Grant Grove** Restaurant. **Cedar Grove** Limited menu food service (summer only). Order at counter; tables provided.

Camping Campgrounds are shown on the park map on pages 108-109. They operate on a first-come, first-served basis except Lodgepole Campground, which is on the MISTIX reservation system from mid-May to Labor Day. Read the general camping information here; then, if you choose to make a reservation, call MISTIX at 1-800-365-CAMP to reserve a site at Lodgepole. All campgrounds in the parks have tables, fire grills, drinking water, garbage cans, and either flush or pit toilets. A "Campground Information" brochure is available free at visitor centers or by mail.

Sequoia National Park Campgrounds and number of sites: In the **Giant Forest/Lodgepole Area**, Dorst 218 (summer only) and Lodgepole 260. In the **Foothills Area** Potwisha 44, Buckeye Flat 28 (summer only), and South Fork 13. In the **Mineral King Area** (summer only) Atwell Mill 23 and Cold Springs 37.

Kings Canyon National Park Campgrounds and number of sites: In the **Grant Grove Area** Azalea 118, Sunset 184 (summer only), and Crystal Springs 67 (summer only). In the **Cedar Grove Area** (summer only) Sentinel 83, Moraine 120, Sheep Creek 111, and Canyon View 37.

Campgrounds in the parks provide settings from the foothills at 2,100 feet in elevation to mixed-conifer forests at 7,500 feet in elevation. Lodgepole, Atwell Mill, and Grant Grove campgrounds are near giant sequoia groves. There are no campgrounds right under big trees in the parks.

Most people first ask: "What is the nicest campground?" Unfortunately, even the most savvy park ranger cannot answer that question *for you*. Significant differences in campground sizes and settings may prove important to you. If you love the foothills environment, try Potwisha or Buckeye Flat campgrounds. They are warmer than higher-elevation campgrounds and are usually snow-free year round. Potwisha is also attractive if you have a large rig or motor home and don't want to negotiate the General's Highway. Buckeye Flat is for tent camping only.

Cold Springs campground, near the end of the Mineral King Road, is at 7,500 feet in elevation. Its proximity to most Mineral King trailheads means that it fills on Fridays and Saturdays on summer weekends because backpackers use it as a launch point.

National Forest Campgrounds

There are several campgrounds in the national forests surrounding these parks. For information on Hume Lake, Princess, and other Sequoia National Forest campgrounds, call 784-1500. For information on Sierra National Forest campgrounds, including those at Pine Flat and Shaver Lake, call 487-5155. For areas along the east side of the parks, call Inyo National Forest, (619) 873-5841.

Group Campsites (summer only)

There are two group camping areas in Kings Canyon National Park: Sunset Campground in Grant Grove and Canyon View Campground in Cedar Grove. Minimum and maximum group sizes per site are 12/20 and 20/40, respectively. In Sequoia National Park, group sites are found at Dorst Campground. Minimum group size is 15, maximum 75. Sites are available to organizations on a reservation-by-mail basis only. Telephone *inquiries* may be made. Mail reservation requests for sites in Kings Canyon either to Sunset Campground— Group Sites, or to Canyon View Campground—Group Sites, P.O. Box 948, Kings Canyon National Park, CA 93633. To reserve group sites in Sequoia, write to Dorst Campground— Group Sites, Lodgepole Ranger Station, Box C, Sequoia National Park, CA 93262.

National Forest Group Campsites

Sequoia National Forest has four group campgrounds near the parks in its Hume Lake District. These accommodate groups of 50 to 100 people. For reservations call MISTIX, 1-800-283-CAMP after 8 a.m. Pacific time.

Firewood Only dead and down wood may be gathered for use as firewood only. Campfire permits are not required in automobile campgrounds. Please be careful with fire. Extinguish your fire when leaving your campsite. Complete campground regulations and conditions of use are posted in campgrounds and are available at visitor centers.

Camping Regulations Camping is permitted only in designated sites in campgrounds, or in backcountry areas by permit. A maximum of six persons and one vehicle is allowed per campsite, except two vehicles in Potwisha. Fees are charged at all campgrounds as long as water and trash pickup are available. The camping limit from June 14 to September 14 is 14 days, either in a single period or combined separate periods, with a limit of 30 days total per year.

Sanitary Disposal Stations Sanitary disposal stations for RVs and trailers operate year-round in the Potwisha and Grant Grove areas, from Memorial Day to mid-October in Lodgepole, and May to mid-October in Cedar Grove.

Bear Habitat All campers take note: black bears inhabit these parks and may enter campgrounds and other areas humans also use. Foodstuffs **must** be stored and disposed of properly at all times as prescribed by regulations available at visitor centers and on bulletin boards. Use food lockers and bear-proof garbage cans where provided. For the sake of the animals, the National Park Service seeks to maintain bears' natural foraging patterns by eliminating unnatural sources of food. Your cooperation is vital to our success and the well-being of the bears.

A recent survey shows that the average visitor to national parks never gets more than 300 feet from his or her car. That is one-seventeenth of a mile. Within that range you can see—but not walk around—the world's largest living thing and spectacular mountain scenery. Walk a little farther—1,056 feet is one-fifth of a mile—and whole new worlds open up to you, including possible remedies for much that may trouble you in your workaday world. To pick a walk, hike, or backcountry adventure tailored to your interests and physical condition, ask the advice of a ranger at a visitor center.

Trails Sequoia Natural History Association and the National Park Service have produced area maps for Giant Forest, Lodgepole/Wolverton, Mineral King, Grant Grove, and Cedar Grove. Sold at visitor centers, these inexpensive maps provide a brief introduction to each area and narrative descriptions of some of its popular and interesting trails. Distance, walking time, climb, type of walk, and trail characteristics are listed for each trail. For example, from the Grant Grove map, "**General Grant Tree Trail**: distance, round trip .5 mile; time, round trip ½ hour; climb, 30 feet; type of walk, easy, accessible to the handicapped." And from the Giant Forest map, "**Moro Rock/Soldiers Trail Loop**: distance (loop) 6 miles; average time, 4 hours; physical difficulty, moderate; starting point, Giant Forest Village; look for the sign located 30 yards west of the cafeteria."

High Sierra Trail Beginning at Crescent Meadow in the Giant Forest, the High Sierra Trail runs for 70 miles across the Sierra to the top of Mt. Whitney, highest point in the contiguous United States. The trail was designed and built—by hand—between 1927 and 1932. All 70 miles are not for everyone, but you can sample the trail from the Crescent Meadow Road parking lot in a 1.2-mile round trip walk to Eagle View. For vicarious enjoyment of this historic trail, and a nice souvenir, buy a copy of *The High Sierra Trail* guide and history at a visitor center.

John Muir Trail and Pacific Crest Trail Two exciting long-distance trails merge in Sequoia National Park and traverse Kings Canyon National Park on their way north up the Sierra spine to Yosemite National Park and Canada. The John Muir Trail connects Mt. Whitney in Sequoia National Park with the Mist Trail out of the Valley in Yosemite National Park. Most of the trail lies above 7,000 feet in elevation; the portion on Mt. Whitney exceeds 14,000 feet. Best travel times are between July 15 and September 15. Even in August packstock sometimes cannot negotiate snow-laden high passes. Permits are required for overnight stays in the backcountry of the national parks and in national forest wilderness areas. (See **Trip Planning and Permits,** page 118.) Possession of firearms is prohibited in national parks and discouraged in national forests except during hunting season. The Pacific Crest Trail, which runs more than 2,000 miles from Mexico to Canada, enters Sequoia National Park near Siberian Pass south of Mt. Whitney. West of Mt. Whitney it joins the John Muir Trail, staying with it to Yosemite. For trip planning information on these trails, write to Backcountry Permits at the parks' address listed on page 110.

Commercial Guides Commercial guides provide backcountry outfitting and/or experiences for backpackers, skiers, and mountaineers. Write to the parks for a free current list.

Safe and Sensible Hiking All hikers should read and heed the tips and warnings on these two pages. Please remember: all overnight backcountry use requires a backcountry permit.

Athletic shoes and heavy socks may suffice on some trails, but sturdier footgear is recommended. Non-skid hiking shoes or boots serve you best. Stay on the trails.

Learn and practice no-trace backcountry hiking and camping techniques. Short-cutting is dangerous and causes damage from erosion. Dogs and other pets are prohibited on all trails. (See **Pets** under **Management Concerns and Safety Tips**, page 123.) Bicycles and motorcycles and other motor vehicles are prohibited on trails.

Smoking while traveling on trails is prohibited. You may smoke while stopped—clear an area for ashes and carry out all cigarette butts and matches. Do not drink untreated water and do not contaminate lakes and streams. Dispose of human waste properly. Carry out all trash.

Horses and mules have the right-of-way on all trails. As stock approaches you, step to the downhill side of the trail, if possible, and stay quiet while the animals pass. Don't try to touch them.

Check on trail conditions at visitor centers or information stations. High-country trails may remain closed by snow well after summer arrives in the foothills.

Trip Planning and Permits *Backcountry Basics*, a newsletter to help you plan hiking trips, is available free; call or write to the parks for a copy. More information about backcountry use in the parks will be supplied with your backcountry permit. Read this material carefully for your safety and to avoid frustration with logistics. Some permits are available on a first-come, first-served basis, and some may be reserved by mail only. To apply for a backcountry permit you must list **1**. Your entry and exit dates, **2**. Entry and exit trailheads, **3**. Method of travel (foot, horse, ski), **4**. Number of persons in group, **5**. Number of pack and saddle stock, and **6**. Overnight camp areas with number of nights per camp. Send this information to Backcountry Permits at the parks' address. The permit will be issued at the visitor center or ranger station closest to your trailhead.

Camping near your selected trailhead the night before departure may not be possible, particularly if you arrive late the night before at Lodgepole or Mineral King. Campgrounds there fill nearly every night in summer, and you may not camp at the trailhead. Except on holiday weekends, campsites are usually available at Grant Grove and Cedar Grove and at national forest campgrounds outside the parks. **Camping is allowed in designated campgrounds only. It is generally not permitted in the backcountry within less than three miles of trailheads or developed areas.** Check for details before departing.

Water Warning *Giardia lamblia*, a protozoan, may contaminate any surface water, no matter how clean it looks. Drink only water from approved public supplies, or water that has been boiled for 3 to 5 minutes. Iodine and chlorine tablets are not as effective as heat but use iodine tablets if boiling is not possible. If you use a water filter, be certain that it has the correct pore size for filtering *Giardia*. Feces of humans and some domestic and wild animals carry *Giardia*. To help prevent transmission of this and other diseases, bury your waste at least four to six inches deep and at least 100 feet from any water or watercourse, even if it is dry while you are there.

Bear Warning Your backcountry permit packet includes instructions on bear-proof food storage facilities and hanging your food to prevent bears from getting it. Make sure that everyone in your party reads this information before your trip. Do not leave food or coolers in your vehicle at the trailhead. Violations of federal laws requiring proper food storage in bear habitat carry fines of up to $500 and/or imprisonment. The National Park Service is committed to protecting bears and people by segregating bears and human food sources; the law is vigorously enforced.

Hypothermia Danger See **Winter Activities** (page 121) for important information on this all-season killer. Hypothermia can occur even when air temperatures are as high as 50°F.

Theft Thefts do occur in the parks. Lock your car. Don't leave valuables visible; it's best to lock valuables in the trunk.

Stock Use Recreational use of horses, mules, burros, and llamas is appropriate in much of Sequoia and Kings Canyon National Parks. Wilderness regulations and other provisions listed above apply. Write to the parks' address for current grazing and livestock regulations. Included with the regulations is information for trip planning, on the trail, around camp, and after your trip. Some forage areas may not open until July 15 or later. Overnight use requires a backcountry permit. For heavily used areas you may want to reserve your backcountry permit in advance. **Note**: No stock may be held overnight in developed areas unless boarded with a commercial pack station. Arrangements must be made in advance. Stock and riders with limited mountain experience may have trouble in the parks' backcountry, most of which lies above 7,500 feet in elevation. A list of commercial packers is available by writing to the parks' address.

Rock Climbing Very little rock climbing is done in the parks, and there is no published climber's guide. Many routes require lengthy approaches into remote and seldom traveled areas. Permits are not required for climbing, but backcountry permits are required for overnight camping and bivouacs made on climbs. For more information write to the parks or call the backcountry permits number on page 110.

As much as 90 percent of annual precipitation in the southern Sierra occurs between November and April. Most of this falls between January and March, and above 4,000 to 5,000 feet in elevation, most of it as snow. Snow often stays on the ground into May, bringing out crosscountry skiers, snowshoers, and snow play enthusiasts. It can be a time of great outdoor beauty and fun for those who are well prepared and safety conscious. If you are not both, think again before tackling winter here.

Snowshoe walk

For winter warmth dress in layers of wool, silk, or synthetics and wear warm gear on head, hands, and feet. Carry at least two quarts of water and do not consume alcohol. Hiking in snow and snowshoeing are far more strenuous than normal walking. Check with a ranger for trail, avalanche, and weather conditions before you set out.

Winter activities in these parks center around Giant Forest, Grant Grove, and Wolverton. Facilities and services are outlined in the *Sequoia Bark*, the free park newspaper. **Visitor centers** are open daily at Ash Mountain, Lodgepole, and Grant Grove. See page 110 for phone numbers of recordings for information, weather, and road conditions. For information on Grant Grove only, call 335-2856. **Giant sequoia trees** can be seen close up. Parking areas near the General Sherman and General Grant trees are kept plowed. **Evening programs** are offered on weekends at Lodgepole Visitor Center or in Giant Forest at Beetle Rock Center. At Grant Grove they are offered on weekends at the visitor center. Check bulletin boards or visitor centers for day, time, and location. Additional programs may be offered on holidays.

Hiking is usually available on low-elevation trails free of snow in the

Marble Fork at Lodgepole

Pear Lake Trail

Potwisha, Hospital Rock, and South Fork areas of Sequoia National Park. Please remember that backcountry permits are required for all overnight trips. **Snowshoe walks** led by naturalists are offered, conditions permitting, between mid-December and mid-April. Reservations are recommended because snowshoes are provided and numbers are limited. Call the visitor centers for details. **Snow play** areas are located at Wolverton in the Giant Forest area and at Big Stump and Azalea Campground at Grant Grove. You may use sleds, inner tubes, or platters, but remember that tubes, platters, and toboggans cannot be steered. Use caution and supervise children. **Ski touring centers** are open at Wolverton and Grant Grove daily. They offer instructors, lessons, and equipment rentals. Trails abound for varied experience levels. **Cross-country ski trails** are marked connecting Giant Forest, Wolverton, and Lodgepole with scenic points of interest. Grant Grove trails connect with those in Sequoia National Forest. Get maps at visitor centers and ski centers. All overnight snowshoe or ski trips require a backcountry permit, available at ranger stations. There are ski trails at Wolverton for all ability levels, and some of the trails there are being groomed. First aid and comfort stations are also available there. The park concessioner operates a snack bar, retail shops, and rental shop and offers ski instruction. Check on days and hours of operation.

Campgrounds and Lodgings Campgrounds operate first-come, first-served in winter. Several are closed. Available campgrounds and their elevations are: **Potwisha**, 2,100, 3 miles above Ash Mountain, sanitary dump station, open all year (fee). **Lodgepole**, 6,700, parking area only plowed (no fee after significant snowfall). At Grant Grove only the parking area and one loop of **Azalea** campground, 6,500, are plowed (fee). **South Fork**, 3,600, has no piped water or garbage removal in winter. Use bear boxes where provided even in winter. **Giant Forest Lodge** just north of Giant Forest Village offers varied motel and cabin accommodations. **Grant Grove Lodge** offers rustic cabins with bath and housekeeping cabins at Grant Grove Village. Call the Sequoia Guest Services phone number on page 110 for information and reservations and to check on food services.

Winter Driving Tips Carry tire chains in winter. They will be required whenever conditions warrant. Failure to heed the "Chains Required" signs can result in an accident and a citation. To slow down in icy or snowy conditions, lightly feather your brakes. Jamming on brakes causes your vehicle to lose traction. Watch out for snowplows: they may appear at any time and may move against traffic. If you meet a plow, don't make sudden moves. Watch for visual signals or direction from the operator. Antifreeze protection to minus 25°F is recommended.

Carbon monoxide poisoning If fuel-burning stoves, lanterns, or heaters are used in campers, pickups, motor homes, trailers, or closed tents, carbon monoxide poisoning can occur and be fatal.

Hypothermia danger Hypothermia is the lowering of the body's core temperature when the body loses heat faster than it can produce it. Potentially fatal, hypothermia can strike even in summer when wetness and wind compound the effects of cool air. Hypothermia takes more human lives yearly than does any other single outdoor hazard. Symptoms develop fast; as they progress you become less capable of realizing their significance. Hands and feet become numb as blood is diverted to vital organs. This results in uncontrollable shivering, fumbling, and drowsiness. Without proper treatment and warming for the victim, the next stages are stupor, collapse, and death. Stay dry, seek shelter from wind, avoid exhaustion, snack frequently on lots of high-energy foods, and wear a wool cap. Learn how to treat hypothermia before departing.

Persons 16 years of age and older must have a valid California fishing license. State regulations apply and are supplemented by special regulations. Fishing licenses may be purchased in developed areas of the parks, but availability varies. Fishing regulations in the parks are intended to help restore the pristine distribution and abundance of native species.

Bait restrictions apply. Freshwater fish, amphibians, and non-preserved fish eggs (fresh roe) may not be used as bait. Gathering any natural bait, including worms and insects, is prohibited in the parks.

Regulations regarding the same species of fish may vary from location to location within or between the parks. **This makes it very important that you get and read current fishing regulations**, which are available at visitor centers and ranger stations. Park waters contain non-native brown, brook, golden, and rainbow trout as well as native rainbow and Little Kern golden trout. There are also golden trout/ rainbow trout hybrids.

Many of the high-elevation lakes that were barren of fish after the Ice Age were stocked beginning in the 1800s. No waters in the parks are stocked now, in keeping with the National Park Service's philosophy of maintaining natural ecosystems.

Please read and heed the following guidelines and regulations as well as those listed under specific activities elsewhere in this handbook.

Dangerous Rivers With winding, steep roads and even steeper cliffs prevalent, you might assume that traffic accidents and falls would be the foremost killers in these parks. Not so. Most of the few fatalities that occur here from other than natural causes are drownings. The rushing rivers can be as misleading as assumptions. **Respect these rivers regardless of season or water levels.** Streamside rocks are smooth and can cause you to slip into the swift, cold water. Cold water quickly saps your body strength, making it nearly impossible to get out.

Safe Driving Downshift on hills so you don't burn out your transmission when going uphill or your brakes when going downhill. Pull into a safe turnout to look at scenery. All slower-moving vehicles, including RVs, should pull over to let traffic pass. And buckle up for safety — it's the law. Park only in designated turnouts and parking areas. Chains may be required on some park roads at any time in winter.

Wildlife All natural systems in the parks are protected by law. This includes wildlife. Keep a respectful distance so their natural routines are not disturbed. Feeding *any* wildlife is illegal — and dangerous. Small animals may bite and can carry diseases. The parks are home to black bears; proper food storage practices are required by law. Use bear-proof food lockers where provided and use bear-proof garbage cans. Keep a clean camp; don't leave refuse or unattended food in camp at any time. Read and heed the **Bear Warning** on page 119. If your property is damaged or a bear is acting aggressively or obtaining food, please report the incident immediately to a ranger station. If you encounter a bear or a cougar, keep your distance. If it approaches you, make loud noises and throw stones in its direction, but use good judgment. **Do not run or crouch.** Pick up small children. Ask a ranger for more information about how to behave in cougar habitat.

Pets For the sake of wildlife and visitors in the parks, pets must be kept under physical restraint at all times: in an automobile or cage or on a leash less than six feet in length. *Pets may not run loose at any time.* Leaving a pet unattended and tied to an object is prohibited. Ask at a visitor center or ranger station for pet information regarding sanitation, noises, and other concerns. Dogs and other pets are not permitted on trails or in any buildings for general public use. Pets are forbidden on any trails, including the stairway and top of Moro Rock, in the General Sherman Tree area, Beetle Rock area, General Grant Tree area, and the trail to Crystal Cave. Pets running at large in these parks may be destroyed.

Fire Management Congress has directed the National Park Service to perpetuate the natural environment and the processes that created it. Fire is one of these processes. Since 1964 the parks' fire management program has sought to recreate fire's beneficial effects and to restore more natural conditions. Under controlled conditions fire is used to remove fuel accumulations and to restore more natural conditions. These fires will be indicated by signs and need not be reported.

Devils Postpile National Monument

Devils Postpile is a formation of columnar basalt on the Middle Fork of the San Joaquin River. Glaciers quarried away one side of the Postpile, exposing a sheer wall of columns 60 feet high. At its base lie fallen columns jumbled like posts having three to seven sides. The river's Rainbow Falls drops 101 feet. Devils Postpile lies west of U.S. 395 near Mammoth Lakes. Closed in winter. For information write to: Superintendent, Devils Postpile National Monument, P.O. Box 501, Mammoth Lakes, CA 93546.

Devils Postpile

Yosemite National Park   Some of the world's most compactly startling scenery awaits visitors to Yosemite National Park and its Glacier Point. Yosemite Valley's sheer granite walls rise as much as 3,000 feet above its surprisingly level floor. John Muir's Yosemite experiences made him a pioneering advocate of wildlands preservation and animal rights. Yosemite harbors several groves of giant sequoia trees. Yosemite can be reached by car from Mono Lake on the east and the San Francisco Bay Area and Fresno on the west. For information about the park write to: Superintendent, Yosemite National Park, P.O. Box 577, Yosemite National Park, CA 95389.

Yosemite Valley

The Sequoia Natural History Association sells books, maps, art prints, notecards, games, and videotapes on park subjects in the parks and by mail. For a free list of these items, ask at a visitor center or write to: Sequoia Natural History Association, Ash Mountain Box 10, Three Rivers, CA 93271, or call 209-565-3758. Here is a select list of books:

Arno, Stephen. *Discovering Sierra Trees*. 1973.

Dilsaver, Lary M. and William C. Tweed. *Challenge of the Big Trees*. 1990.

Elsasser, A.D. *Indians of Sequoia and Kings Canyon*. 1988.

Grater, Russell. *Discovering Sierra Mammals*. 1978.

Harvey, H.T. and others. *The Giant Sequoia*. 1981.

Hill, Mary. *Geology of the Sierra Nevada*. 1975.

Oberhansley, Frank. *Crystal Cave*. 1984.

Palmer, John. *In Pictures, Sequoia and Kings Canyon: The Continuing Story*. 1990.

Rockwell, Jack and Stephen Stocking. *Wildflowers of Sequoia and Kings Canyon National Parks*. 1989.

Starr, Walter. *Starr's Guide to the John Muir Trail*. 1974.

Storer, Tracy I. and Robert L. Usinger. *Sierra Nevada Natural History*. 1963.

Strong, Douglas. *Trees or Timber?* 1986.

Tweed, William C. *Exploring Mountain Highways*. 1984.

Tweed, William C. *Kaweah Remembered*. 1986.

Tweed, William C. *Sequoia and Kings Canyon: The Story Behind the Scenery*. 1989.

Wheelock, Walt and Tom Condon. *Climbing Mount Whitney*. 1989.

Whitney, Stephen. *A Sierra Club Naturalist's Guide to the Sierra Nevada*. 1979.

☆ GPO: 1991—281-952/40002

Index

Numbers in italics refer to photographs, illustrations, or maps

Agriculture 15, 44, *46-47*
Agriculture, U.S. Department of 20
Animals *38-39, 54-59, 92-93.* See also under individual species
Army, U.S. *74-75,* 77, 79

Backpacking 86-87, 95, 103, *113, 117*
Bears 94, 115, 119; grizzly *56-57,* 87; black *56-57, 59,* 87, 94, *98*
Big Trees. See Sequoia tree, Giant
Bio-ethics 21
Biosphere Reserve 21
Birds *38-39, 58-59,* 92, 93
Blanchard, Smoke 86
Brewer, Mount 78
Brewer, William 79
Brown, Bolton Coit 78
Buena Vista, Lake 44

California *37, 46-47, 96-97;* Conservation Corps *91;* tree *66.* See also San Joaquin Valley
Cave *88-89*
Cedar Grove 33
Challenge of the Big Trees 33, 87
Chaparral *36, 38-39,* 50
Civilian Conservation Corps, U.S. *75*
Clark, Henry B. 76
Clyde, Norman 85-*87,* 103
Cohen, Michael 11, 103
Conservation, Utilitarian 20, 21, 50. See also Development, private
Crystal Cave *88-89*

Darwin, Charles 21
Development, private 61, 62, *72-73*
Devils Postpile National Monument *124*

Dicentra 39
Dilsaver, Lary M. 33, 87
Douglas William O. 20
Dragonfly *58*
Dusy Basin *90-91*

Ecosystem 50, *64-65,* 98, *100-101;* aquatic policy 94; definition 37; effects of fire 68-69, 71, *80-81;* Giant Sequoia tree *64-65;* San Joaquin Valley 14-15, 20-21; thwarted development *72-73*
Ed by Ned tree *67*
Eleven Range Overlook 96
Ewell, Diane *98*

Fir *42,* 80
Fire, forest *68-69, 80, 81*
Fish *48-49,* 94, 122-23
Fisher *54-55*
Fodor, Paul 94-95
Forests *40-41*
Fox, John 35
Fox: gray *58;* Sierra Nevada red *54-55*
Fresno: County 44; Eddy *97*
Frog, foothill yellow-legged *49*
Fry, Walter 74

General Grant National Park 34, 74, 76; origin 15, 20; tourism 78-79. See also Kings Canyon National Park
General Land Office, U.S. 61
Generals Highway *4-5,* 36
Geographic Information System *100-101*
Giant Forest 35, 36, 70, *78;* precipitation 41; roads in 74, 77; Sequoia National Park 61, 62, 95
Global warming, signs of 54
Goldman Fund 52
Graber, David 54, 61, 87, 94, 98
Grant tree, General 15, *66*
Great Basin 40
Great Western Divide *40,* 62

High Sierra Trail 70, 116
Hough, Emerson *95*

Huxley, Mount *30-31*
Hydrick, Rick 70-71
Hydroelectric power 44-45, 46, 50

Kaweah: Colony 61; River 36, 44, 45, 46
Kearsarge Pass 72
Keith, William 15
Kern: County 44; River 44, 46; Valley *100-101*
King, Clarence 79
Kings: Canyon *18-19,* 33, 34, 35; Highway 36; River 33, 44, 45; River Canyon *32,* 36, *37*
Kings Canyon National Park 20, 48, 78, 80; ecological benefits 15, 20-21, 29, 44, 45, 50; elevation 36; founding 33-34, 35; hydroelectric power 45, 50; illustrations *2-3, 6-7, 20, 24-25, 29, 90-91, back cover;* map *20, 108-9.* See also Grant National Park; Tourist information

LeConte, Joseph N. 78
Legislation 15
Log Meadow *28*
Lovelace, Joseph W. "Shorty" 55
Lyon, Thomas J. 11

Manzanita *51*
Marble Fork *120*
Marten *54-55*
Mather, Stephen T. *95*
Medley, A.L. 89
Mineral King 15, 20, *73,* 77, 78, *84*
Moro Rock *10, 72, 76,* 77, 96, *97*
Muir, John 11, 14, 15, 21, 29, 33, *35,* 50, 64; Hut *113;* Trail 78, 116

National Geographic Magazine 96
National Park Service 79; management policies 57, 63, 74-75, 94, 95, 103; reasons for creation 15, 20-21, 29
Nichols, Tom 71, 80

Oak: black *38-39;* blue *38-39*
Ozone pollution 37, 96. *See also* Pollution, air

Pacific Crest Trail 116
Parsons, David 99
Pathless Way, The 103
Pear Lake *120*
Pine: foxtail *43,* height 80; lodgepole *26-27,* 29; ponderosa *42,* 96; sugar *42*
Plants 28, *38-39,* 50, *51, 82-83, 90-93. See also* Chaparral; Sequoia tree, Giant; Trees
Pollution, air 14, 37, *96-97*
Precipitation 40-41, 45, 46; acid 37, *99. See also* snowpack

Rae Lakes 48
Redwood, coast *63*
Robinson, Charles D. 34
Round Meadow 77

San Joaquin Valley 15, 20-21, 29, 46, 47, 96-97
Sequoia and Kings Canyon National Parks Foundation 110
Sequoia Natural History Association 88, 110, 111
Sequoia National Park *22-23,* 74, 76, 77, 79; ecological benefits 15, 20-21, 29, 44, 45, 50; elevation 36; founding 15, 20, 62; hydroelectric power 45; Kern Canyon 36; lakes and ponds 48; map *20, 108-9;* management policies 63, 70-71; *See also* Giant Forest; Tourist information
Sequoia tree, Giant 15, 71, 80; photos *front cover, 4-5, 36, 60, 62, 64-69, 81*
Se-quo-yah *44*
Sheep: domestic 90; bighorn *52-53, 59, 93*
Sherman tree, General *60,* 61, *113*
Sierra Club 35, 73, *76-77,* 78
Sierra Crest *41*
Sierra Forest Reserve 35
Sierra Nevada *36-37, 46-47, 65*
Silliman Crest 97

Snowpack *46-47,* 96
Solomons, Theodore 78
Southern Sierra Research Center 87
Spanish Mountain 36
Squirrel, Douglas (Chickaree) *65*
Stanford, Mount *6-7*
Stegner, Wallace 15, 29
Stewart, George 20, 46, 61-63, *70*
Stewart, Mount 62
Swetnam, Thomas 99

Tehipite Valley 15, 45
Tharp, Hale *45,* 61, 111
Tokopah Falls *104-5*
Tourism, oldtime *76-79*
Tourist Information:
   Disabilities services 110
   Education programs 112
   Golden Age Passports 111
   Fishing 122-23
   Hiking and backpacking *113,* 116, *117,* 118
   Health and safety 118-19, 121-22, 123
   Lodging and camping 110, 114-15, 119, 121
   Map *108-9*
   Nature center 112
   Park newspaper 110
   Pets 123
   Ranger stations 111-12
   Religious services 110
   Skiing *113,* 116, 118
   Snowshoe walks *120,* 121
   Transportation 106-7, 121
   Visitor centers 111
   Weather 107
Trees *26-27,* 29, *41-43,* 62, *63, 99. See also* Sequoia tree, Giant
Tulare: Basin 44; County 44, 77
Tweed, William C. 33, 34, 63, 70, 87

Visalia 77

Webster, C. N. 89
Wheelock, Walt 85

White, Fay 70
White, John Roberts 62, 63, *70-*71, 79
Whitney, Mount 35, 63, 70, 86; illustrations *16-17, 22-23, 37;* Military Reservation 15
Wilderness 20, 85; Act of 1964 95
Wildflowers *See* Plants
Wildlife *See* Animals
Wolverine *54-55*

Yellowstone National Park 21
Yokuts Indians 62
Yosemite National Park 78, *124*
Young, Charles *45, 111*
Yucca *51*

National Park Service

The National Park Service expresses its appreciation
to all those people who made the preparation and
production of this volume possible. Special thanks
are due the Sequoia Natural History Association.
Unless credited below, photographs and illustrations
come from the files of Sequoia and Kings Canyon
National Parks and the National Park Service. Some
are restricted against reproduction.